Patricia Hill Collins

Reconceiving Motherhood

Patricia Hill Collins

Reconceiving Motherhood

Edited by

Kaila Adia Story

DEMETER PRESS

Demeter Press
140 Holland Street West
P. O. Box 13022
Bradford, ON L3Z 2Y5
Tel: (905) 775-9089
Email: info@demeterpress.org
Website: www.demeterpress.org

Demeter Press logo based on the sculpture "Demeter" by Maria-Luise Bodirsky <www.keramik-atelier.bodirsky.de>

Printed and Bound in Canada

Library and Archives Canada Cataloguing in Publication

Patricia Hill Collins : reconceiving motherhood / Kaila Adia Story, ed.

Includes bibliographical references.
ISBN 978-1-927335-43-7 (pbk.)

1. Hill Collins, Patricia. 2. Motherhood. 3. African American mothers. 4. Feminism. I. Story, Kaila Adia, 1980-, editor

HQ759.P37 2014 306.874'3 C2014-906520-5

This book is dedicated to my ancestors,
for their guidance and protection.
To my brilliant parents, Sylvia Rogers and Dr. Ralph Story
whose courage, support, love, and guidance allowed me
to envision, create, and complete this book.
To my grandmother, Mo, whose wisdom and insight
remains a reservoir of strength in my life.
To my partner Missy, for her encouragement,
support and unyielding love, and to my
Feminist sister for whom this work exists.
This is for you.

Table of Contents

Acknowledgements
ix

Motherhood as a Praxis, Institution, and Lived Experience:
A Brief Introduction
Kaila Adia Story
1

Multiracial Motherhood: A Genealogical Exploration
Sarah N. Gatson
13

Patricia Hill Collins as Pedagogical Mother
Abigail L. Palko
38

Mothering Past the Line of No Defense:
Millennial Daughters on the Path to Crafting
a Black Feminism of Their Own
Toni C. King and S. Alease Ferguson
56

Other mothers in Motion:
Conceptualizing African American Stepmothers
Deidre Hill Butler
78

Black Motherhood and The Power of the
Intersectionality Framework:
A Midwifery Perspective on the "New Racism"
Karline Wilson-Mitchell and Vincia Herbert
97

Sympathetic Distances of Black Motherhood:
Reflections on the Political Agency of Cultural Remembering
Shelley Grant
122

Nineteenth-Century Motherwork:
Ideology, Experience, and Agency in Autobiographical
Narratives by Black Women
Martha Pitts
142

Situated Knowledge—Coming to Voice, Coming to Power:
The Mothers Committee of Bayview Hunters
Nancy Arden McHugh
160

Living My Material:
An Interview with Patricia Hill Collins
Kaila Adia Story
181

Contributor Notes
192

Acknowledgements

I WOULD LIKE TO TAKE THIS OPPORTUNITY to thank those special individuals for their unyielding support throughout this process. To Dr. Andrea O'Reilly, thank so much for inviting me to edit this volume while I was still an unknown Assistant Professor. Your belief in my abilities as a scholar and editor has meant so much. To all of the contributors, whose work is housed in this volume, I thank you so much for your attention to detail, and all of your dedication and consistency throughout this process, you are all truly amazing, and working with you all has been an absolute pleasure. Lastly, I would like to thank Dr. Patricia Hill Collins for her amazing work as a brilliant scholar, public intellectual, and organic activist.

Collins has been, and remains, one of the foremost Black Feminist writers of our time. From the beginning of her writing and academic career, Collins' perspective and approach to her work, has made meaning of the experiences of women and men of African descent. Continuously emphasizing the bearings that race, class, gender, and sexuality have on Black American culture. As a feminist writer who has always gone beyond just focusing on a generalized category known as "women," her research agenda and approach to her published work has always explored the many ways that relations of gender, intersecting with race, class, ethnicity, sexuality, and spirituality, and other "differences" affect every aspect of identity; every aspect of society. In line with her Pan-African perspective, as a feminist, Collins has always argued that analyses of gender must be historically contextualized and challenge us as citizens to re-examine and further question the a priori "fact" of the subordination of women. There is no time like the present to honor Collins work by highlighting it in this volume. Thank you all so much for you.

Motherhood as a Praxis, Institution and Lived Experience

A Brief Introduction

KAILA ADIA STORY

MOTHERHOOD AS A PRAXIS, institution, and lived experience has been discussed by a myriad of scholars in general and specific ways. The dominant portrayal of what is, and what it means to be a "mother," however, remains locked within a reductive and imaginary prism of white supremacy, heteronormativity, and sexism. Feminist scholarship in conjunction with motherhood studies has expanded, and continues to expand, our own analysis as citizens of what motherhood actually looks like within a lived context. Through this scholarship and activism, new definitions and terms have been created, and the freedom around the institution and praxis of motherhood and mothering has also expanded. Patricia Hill Collins has given new meaning to the institution of motherhood throughout her publishing career. Introducing scholars to new concepts, such as, "othermothering" and "mothering of the mind," Collins' creative and multifaceted analysis of the institution of motherhood, has in a sense, reconceived what it means to be a mother in a national and transnational context. By connecting motherhood as an institution to manifestations of empire, racism, classism, and heteronormativity, Collins has informed and invented new understandings of the institution as a whole.

Since the 1990 release of *Black Feminist Thought: Knowledge, Consciousness, and the Politics of Empowerment*, Patricia Hill Collins has been articulating an alternative view of black womanhood within the academy and beyond. Her epistemological specificity, illuminates the non-complacement and resistant tradition of Black and Female scholarship, activism, and research. This groundbreaking book, not only sought to teach us about the social construction of Black Feminist thought, the controlling images of Black womanhood, and the importance of self definition as a means to empowerment for Black women, but Patricia Hill Collins also, discussed at length the necessity of re-examining the institution of motherhood, by utilizing an intersectional analysis. Realizing that women shared a history with one another, through the material conditions of sexuality and reproduction, and that African Americans shared a history with one another through systems of domination, Collins highlighted that Black women had a specific standpoint by which they viewed the world. This standpoint, rich in alternative epistomology, engendered a ritualistic practice of open-ended discourse within the academy and society about the place of Black women. "Feminist work on motherhood from the 1970s and 1980s produced a limited critique of these views. Reflecting White, middle-class women's angles of vision, feminist analyses typically lacked an adequate race amd class analysis" (*Black Feminist Thought* 173). Conversely,

> ...many African American [male] thinkers tend to glorify Black motherhood ... by claiming that Black women are richly endowed with devotion, self-sacrifice, and unconditional love-the attributes associated with archetypal motherhood-U.S. Black men inadvertanly foster a different albeit seemingly positive image for Black women. The controlling image of the "superstrong Black mother" praises Black women's resiliency in a society that routinely paints us as bad mothers. Yet, in order to remain on their pedestal, these same superstrong Black mothers must continue to place their needs behind those of everyone eles, especially their sons. (*Black Feminist Thought* 174)

To Collins, the institution of Black motherhood was saturated with myth, self-policing, and too much outside influence over what it actually meant to be a Black mother in America. One of the major ideological roadblocks within the acadmic exploration of Black motherhood, to Collins, was the enduring popularized caricature of Black mothers—the Mammy.

The figure, born on the plantation in the imagination of slavery defenders, grew in popularity during the beginnings of Jim Crow segregation around 1876. The mainstreaming of the Mammy was primarily, but not exclusively, the result of the fledging advertising industry (Jewell). The Mammy image was used to sell almost any household item, especially breakfast foods, detergents, planters, ashtrays, sewing accessories, and beverages. The mythologized Mammy was so loyal to her White family that she was often willing to risk her life to defend them. Although the visual depictions of her body illustrated ample buttocks and breasts, the Mammy was seen as a non-sexual or asexual figure, whose body was shaped that way to convey her maternal nature and intrinsic ability to care for White children. The figure was strategically positioned this way to show the inherent unattractiveness of Black women and to justify the notion that Black women needed and wanted to be controlled by White families and inevitably, White men.

Although the intital conditions used to define the mammy figure have since been eroded, the perpetual use of the mammy image continues to naturalize itself within the American experience of family. "These controlling images are designed to make racism, sexism, poverty, and other forms of social injustice appear natural, normal, and inevitable parts of everyday life" (Collins *Black Feminist Thought* 69). The continued use of the Mammy image was and is found in both media and television shows, such as the popular show *Beulah*. The show was popular from 1950 to 1953, in which a Mammy nurtures a White suburban family. The "Beulah" image resurfaced again in the eighties television show *Gimmie A Break* in which, the late Nell Carter, a talented Black singer, played a Mammy-like role on the situation comedy. She was a dark-skinned, overweight, sassy, white-identified woman, and like Aunt Delilah in the film *Imitation of Life* (1934), was content to live in her White employer's home and nurture the White family.

"The Matriarch" figure, the flip side of "the Mammy" figure, was used to symbolize "the mother figure in black homes" (Collins *Black Feminist Thought* 75) . The "Matriarch" archetype was also used as an ideological trope to define public policy when it came to Black women and Black families. "The Black matriarchy thesis argued that African American women who failed to fulfill their traditional "womanly" duties at home contributed to social problems in Black civil society" (Collins *Black Feminist Thought* 75). In 1965 a then sociologist and eventual U.S. senator, Daniel Patrick Moynihan released his report, "The Negro Family: The Case for National Action." The report concluded that the Black family existed as a tangle of pathology, which struggled to make progress toward economic and political equality due to its deterioration of the concept of the nuclear family. Since the release of the report, Collins and other Black feminists and motherhood scholars have elucidated the ways in which Moynihan's conception of the Black family, in particular the Black mother, was couched in racist, classist, and sexist notions of the family and the institution of motherhood.

> Spending too much time away from home, these working mothers ostensibly could not properly supervise their children and thus were a major contributing factor to their children's failure at school. As overly aggressive, unfeminine women, Black matriiarchs allegedly emasculated their lovers and husbands. These men, undersatndbly, either deserted their partners or refused to marry the mothers of their children. From a dominant group's perspective, the matriarch represented a failed mammy, a negative stigma to be applied to African American women who dared reject the image of submissive, hardwroking servant. (Collins *Black Feminist Thought* 75)

Contrary to the polualrized images of "The Mammy" and "The Matriarch," Collins saw the actual practice of Black motherhood differently when examining research that had been done for and by black women themselves.

> Black women intellectuals who study African-American families and Black motherhood typically report finding few matriarchs and even fewer mammies. Instead they portray African-American mothers as complex individuals who

> often show tremendous stregnth under adverse conditions, or who become beaten down by the incessant demands of providing for their families. (Collins *Black Feminist Thought* 75-76)

Not only was the instituion of Black motherhood completely different than many theorists have previously argued, but Black motherhood was "both dynamic and dialectical" (Collins *Black Feminist Thought* 176). Not only had Black mothers resisted the hegemonic and racist notions of mainstream society's idea of them, but they also formed and created different types of mothering within Black communities that were not only revolutionary but creative.

"Community Mothering" or "Other Mothering" has been defined as a form of mothering that is rooted in political activism and within a Black Feminist paradigm. It is the concept of accepting responsibility for a child that is not one's own in an arrangement that may or may not be formal. Although motherhood is a contradictory institution experienced in diverse ways by different women. To Collins, Black women have functioned as "community mothers" and "other mothers" for centuries.

> Othermothers can be key not only in supporting children but also in helping bloodmothers who, for whatever reason, lack the preparation or desire for motherhood. In confronting racial oppression, maintain community-based child-care and respecting othermothers who assume child-care responsibilities can serve a critical function in African-American communities. Children orphaned by sale or death of their parents under slavery, children conceived through rape, children of young mothers, children born into extreme poverty or to alcoholic or drug-addicted mothers, or children who for other reasons cannot remain with their bloodmothers have all been supported by othermothers, who...take in additional children even when they have enough of their own. (Collins *Black Feminist Thought* 180)

"Community Mothering" or "Other Mothering" then demonstrates a committed connection to black communities, attending to a socially responsible ethic that is imbued with the idea of political activism to the larger black community. Hill Collins argued that they were reflections of this concept within Black families, dating back to West African societies. To Hill Collins, although enslavement certainly produced "profound changes to Africans enslaved in the United States" (Collins *Black Feminist Thought* 181), enslaved Africans still continued their "beliefs in the importance of motherhood and the value of cooperative approaches to child care continued" (181).

After the publication of her book, *Black Feminist Thought: Knowledge, Consciousness, and the Politics of Empowerment*, Collins went on to publish several books that emphasized Black women's subjectivity, recovered Black women's particular and specific relationship to the state, and continued to write in all of her books with a spirit of justice when it came to Black women, Black families, and Black children. In her 1998 book, *Fighting Words: Black Women and the Search for Justice,* Collins investigates how effectively Black feminist thought, as a theory and standpoint, confronts the injustices that Black women currently face. Collins also argues that the institutions of poverty, mothering, and White supremacy are all reasons that a liberated social theory should also be infused with justice.

In 2005, Patricia Hill Collins wrote *Black Sexual Politics: Africans Americans, Gender, and The New Racism*. In the book, Collins examines the narrow Western view of sexuality and the various ways in which, these ideologues impact the intersectional experience of African Americans. Collins also cautions African Americans to be weary of "the New Racism," new forms of racism that work to oppress Black people, but at the same time are imbued with messages of liberation and empowerment. Lastly, Collins stresses a liberatory politic for African Americans, removed from stereotypes of the past, and imbued with a subjective standpoint that is rooted within the African American experience. Only one year later, From *Black Power to Hip Hop: Racism, Nationalism, Feminism* was released in 2006, and explored and analyzed various issues. In this book, Collins creates a historical genealogy of African American life from late 1960s to the 2000s, and how "The New Racism" has facilitated a myriad of challenges for African Americans who were seeking empowerment in their communities and lives. From *Black Power to Hip Hop* is the first book of its kind to explore the impact of nationalism, feminism, and racism, in the lives of twenty-first century Black Americans.

In 2010, Patricia Hill Collins wrote, *Another Kind of Public Education: Race, Schools, the Media, and Democratic Possibilities*, where she discussed the emerging sentiment of "color blindness" within our country.

> Moreover, in the current, seemingly color-blind context where the next generation of Americans is increasingly of color, the United States must find a way to build a democratic national community with an increasingly heterogeneous population Rather than equating excellence with elitism—the posture that encourages keeping people out—we might define excellence as being compatible with diversity. Only by involving a range of points of view in the democratic process will the United States get the kind of innovation that it needs. (xv)

Collins discusses public education and schools as warehouses where theses ideas are played out. Public education has always been, to Collins, a space, where institutionalized racism, and the power of media have always been entwined. The inherent power of education, especially for young people of color can be a way for them to renegotiate their role as American citizens and revamp the democratic process altogether. *On Intellectual Activism*, which Collins wrote in 2012, challenges public intellectuals, scholars, and activists to rethink the ideological and ontological benefits from speaking truth to power and assessing the true meaning of their work. Further, Collins argues, how we as citizens come to understand, and make meaning out of public intellectual rhetoric, and how this rhetoric is presented. The volume, which consists of Collins' public speeches, previously published essays, and interviews, illustrates her career throughout the decades, all the while, highlighting themes that exist within her many bodies of work.

Patricia Hill Collins is not just a brilliant scholar, public intellectual, and organic activist, she has been, and remains, one of the foremost Black feminist writers of our time. From the beginning of her writing and academic career, Collins' perspective and approach to her work has made meaning of the experiences of women and men of African descent. Continuously emphasizing the bearings that race, class, gender, and sexuality have on Black American culture. As a feminist writer who has always gone beyond just focusing on a generalized category known as "women," her research agenda and approach to her published work has always explored the many ways that relations of gender, intersecting with race, class, ethnicity, sexuality, and spirituality, and other "differences" affect every aspect of identity; every aspect of society. In line with her Pan-African perspective, as a feminist, Collins has always argued that analyses of gender must be historically contextualized and challenge us as citizens to re-examine and further question the a priori "fact" of the subordination of women.

To follow this assumption, to Collins, is to ignore the phenomenology of "womanhood" as it manifests globally and cross-culturally and to further ignore the multiple sites of empowerment and agency exercised by women. Power, in her estimation, is negotiated and negotiable, should be assessed in relative terms, and should be framed within specific historical contexts. In this way, Collins encourages readers to recognize that both gender and power have the ability to take on variable meanings in variable contexts. Rather than focus solely on the ways in which gender serves as a tool of oppression, Patricia Hill Collins has always sought to offer her readers a balanced perspective, multifaceted analysis, and insist that as we speak of oppression we also speak of resistance.

Patricia Hill Collins' interdisciplinary and intersectional work encourages other academics and public intellectuals to be more innovative, creative, and flexible, when approaching their own work. By engaging different lines of questioning simultaneously, students develop the skills to be focused while thinking "outside of the box" through interdisciplinary thinking. In preparing students to meet the greatest challenges of our time, interdisciplinary research and pedagogy allows for and fosters complex thinking, problem solving for the greater intellectual benefit not only to the student but also to the world. This edited collection adds to the existing literature on motherhood and the conceptions of family through critical examinations of Patricia Hill Collins' many works. This collection raises critical questions about the social and cultural meanings of race, class, gender, sexual orientation, and mothering. In the spirit of Demeter Press and the Motherhood Initiative for Research and Community Involvement (MIRCI), the contributors to this volume are honored to have been given the opportunity to discuss the impact/influence/ and/or importance of Patricia Hill Collins on motherhood research.

Sarah N. Gatson's article, "Multiracial Motherhood: A Genealogical Exploration," interweaves narratives about her own encounters with mothering/motherhood and puts forth a discussion of the intellectual genealogy that has informed her scholarship, practice, and scholarship of practice. Gatson contends that critical intellectual formation comes from the "self-conscious struggle" of being mothered, observing mothering, and doing motherhood, as well as through the introduction to key formal concepts as articulated in the works of Patricia Hill Collins. In Abigail Palko's essay, "Patricia Hill Collins as Pedagogical Mother," Palko who has taught Patricia Hill Collins' work in a variety of courses, surveys former students about the impact of reading Collins' works, and interviews graduate students about their own experiences of teaching Collins' works, to propose a new way to explore the works of Hill Collins as a necessary pedagogical tool to understand the institution of motherhood.

In "Mothering Past the Line of No Defense: Millennial Daughters on the Path to Crafting a Black Feminism of Their Own," Toni C. King and Alease Ferguson utilize Collins' paradigmatic questions to interrogate the distinctions between past and present mother-daughterline work, relative to millennial college age daughters, elucidating some of the ways in which, these daughters are finding their way to the Motherline and finding a Black Feminism of their own. Deidre Hill Butler's essay, "Other Mothers in Motion: Conceptualizing African American Stepmothers," discusses how African American stepmothers employ Patricia Hill Collins' othermothering framework in their day to day lives, introducing a comprehensive understanding of the conception of African American stepmothers' lived experiences. Through six in-depth interviews with African American stepmothers from the Northeastern United States, Butler discusses the many challenges and coping mechanisms that African American stepmothers employ to support their stepmother role and further engage the othermothering framework.

In "Black Motherhood and The Power of the Intersectionality Framework: A Midwifery Perspective on the 'New Racism,'" Karline Wilson-Mitchell and Vincia Herbert utilize the language, theoretical rubric, and critical social theory of Patricia Hill Collins to define the intersectionality of oppression, and discuss it within the lived reality of a Black midwife healer, academic, and a person who observes motherhood. This is an extremely important ideological intervention in a postmodern Canada that claims to be a "color-blind" society while institutional racism remains. In Shelley Grant's essay, "Sympathetic Distances of Black Motherhood: Reflections on the Political Agency of Cultural Remembering," Grant examines the political agency of remembering as a product of cultural and private knowledge's about Black motherhood. While deconstructing Collins' work on the intersectionality of race and normative cultural values in the construction of Black family identities, Grant assess the agency of memories to distance Black mothers from valorized and politicized Eurocentric family ideals of maternal "care."

In Martha Pitts' article "Nineteenth-Century Motherwork Ideology, Experience, and Agency in Autobiographical Narratives by Black Women," Pitts articulates how the trope of motherhood as analyzed by scholars in major reclamation work of nineteenth-century has been inextricably tied to whiteness, the "private," and to the blood-related relationships. Further, Pitts contends that nineteenth-century Black mothering has always operated outside of the traditional mother-child model and/or traverses of bloodlines, but, Pitts contends, that this work has been egregiously overlooked; Pitts posits Collins' concept of "othermothering" as potentially productive point of departure when examining this work. Her essay not only corrects this oversight but builds upon Collins' scholarship, broadening its significance to a larger critical discourse on mothering. In Nancy Arden McHugh's essay, "Situated Knowledge-Coming to Voice, Coming to Power: The Mothers Committee of Bayview Hunters," McHugh discusses Patricia Hill Collins' theory on "the politics of containment" in the lives of the women of Bayview Hunters Point. McHugh contends that in spite of their "containment" the women of Bayview Hunters Point refused to let their health, community, and lives go unnoticed. Her essay examines the alternative resources, methods, and coalitions that theses women formed to resist and fight back.

Lastly, on November 22, 2013, I got a chance to sit down with Dr. Patricia Hill Collins, Distinguished University Professor of Sociology at the University of Maryland, College Park, about her research and publications on Motherhood as praxis, an institution, and a lived experience. In "Living My Material: An Interview with Dr. Patricia Hill Collins" (which is presented in this volume in transcript form) we discuss Collins' scholarship in conjunction with her lived experiences as a daughter, mother, other mother, and grandmother to elucidate the ways in which her scholarship and work around motherhood has been inextricably linked to her own personal and academic journeys.

WORKS CITED

Collins, Patrcia Hill. *Fighting Word: Black Women and the Search for Justice.* Minneapolis: University of Minnesota Press , 1998.

Collins, Patricia Hill. *Another Kind of Public Education: Race, Schools, the Media, and Democratic Possibilities.* Boston: Becon Press, 2010.

Collins, Patrcia Hill. *Black Feminist Thought: Knowledge, Consciousness, and the Politics of Empowerment.* New York: Routledge, 2000.

Collins, Patrcia Hill. *Black Sexual Politics: African Americans, Gender, and The New Racism.* New York: Routledge, 2005.

Collins, Patrcia Hill. *From Black Power to Hip Hop: Racism, Nationalism, Feminism.* Philadelphia: Temple University Press, 2006.

Collins, Patrcia Hill. *On Intellectual Activism.* Philadelphia: Temple University Press, 2012.

Jewell, Sue K. *From Mammy to Miss America and Beyond.* New York: Routledge Press, 1992.

Moynihan, Daniel Patrick. "The Negro Family: The Case for

National Action." Washington: Office of Policy Planning and Research, United Stated Department of Labor, March 1965. Web. Accessed July 1, 2014.

Multiracial Motherhood

A Genealogical Exploration

SARAH N. GATSON

AS I WRITE IN MID-SEPTEMBER, 2012, we are looking forward to celebrating the birthday of my cheerful, bright, and healthy son. My choice to become a mother was a choice that was not an inevitable one. First came treatment for endometriosis and miscarriage, followed by a pregnancy complicated by gestational diabetes; surgery to remove a gallbladder; a burst appendix, and later an emergency Cesarean. Likewise, expanding our family has been further complicated by two more miscarriages, including one that required surgical completion after a heartbeat could no longer be detected. At 42, I now await our pre-adoptive home study, hoping someone I have not yet met, suffering from an unimaginable personal crisis, will choose me to be the mother of her child. As much as my motherhood is grounded in these mundanely extraordinary, intensely personal experiences, it is at the same time grounded in my scholarship of culture, history, policy, and the law. Using Patricia Hill Collins's discussion of critical social theory, coupled with a "personalized statement" (Collins "Shifting the Center" 46), the following essay interweaves mothering/motherhood narratives and an analysis of the intellectual genealogy that has informed my scholarship, my practice, my scholarship of practice, and my practice of my scholarship. This critical intellectual formation comes from the "self-conscious struggle" (Collins *Black Feminist Thought* 15) of being mothered, observing mothering, and doing motherhood.

In discussing micro- and macro-level pathways of arranging our lives, Collins uses the term "motherwork" to

> soften the existing dichotomies in feminist theorizing about motherhood that posit rigid distinctions between private and public, family and work, the individual and the collective, identity as individual autonomy and identity growing from the collective self-determination of one's group.... "Work for the day to come," is motherwork, whether it is on behalf of one's own biological children, or for the children of one's own racial ethnic community, or to preserve the earth for those children who are yet unborn. (Collins "Shifting the Center" 15).

This essay, which is a manifestation of motherwork, is an exploration of Collins discussions of the concepts, "outsider within", "standpoint", "intersectionality", "mothering of the mind" (Collins *Black Feminist Thought* 11, 24-25, 18, 198), "othermothering," and "motherwork" through generative connection (see Haraway 81-108) to concepts such as amorphousness (Gatson "On Being Amorphous"; "The Genealogy of Daisy Bates") in a particular analysis of "the themes of survival, power, and identity" (Collins "Shifting the Center" 49) found in a grounded experience of mothering and motherhood scholarship. If "the personal is political," it is also cultural, theoretical, and communal—the self is fundamentally produced within a web of affiliations chosen and un-chosen. Examining our selves, the facets of our self, we may learn that "new selves may incorporate the old self, yet emerge from new situations" (Gatson "Self-naming Practices on the Internet").

VIGNETTE: MOTHERS AND OTHERMOTHERS

I have been Nickey, Nicole, Sarah, SarahNicole, Miss Gatson, Ms. Gatson, Dr. Gatson, Mrs. Quick, but never, ever Sally. Sally was my mother, and our names were distinguished by our middle names. Distinguishing myself from Sarah Louise Gatson has been a constant struggle, between severing destructive bonds with her and embracing her history. Both my own instincts of self-preservation and my developing scholarship led me down a path that was increasingly away from her. I have had to confront her legacy of motherhood, while finding my conscious practices of parenting from a host of othermothers from among my biological and fictive kin. Thinking through the circumstances, events, and individual actions in which I am grounded, is a "way of linking up the world of ideas to which [I am] now professionally tied with the nitty-gritty of [my] daily life" (Narayan 37). Writing professionally as Sarah N. Gatson, I start here with the nitty-gritty of my mother's life, exploring the narratives I have known so well, and the surprises I learned as an adult.

Instead of the sociological concept of identity as "master status," Black feminist theory finds tightly interwoven strands of social meaning, at once conceptually separable and experientially meshed into overarching sets, existing as what Angela Davis has called a "dialectical character" (44).[1] In any such set—"white working-woman" for example—the strands may be teased apart in the examination of the various statuses each strand is formally or culturally granted in particular contexts. Taking my mother as an example: she entered high school in Kansas City, Missouri in 1965. Notes in her yearbook made it clear that from the outset friends considered her active, smart, and popular. Four years later, her yearbook documents how she and my father, in a time-honored American ritual, were voted best-known couple, complete with cute posed photo on the Plaza (*Crusader* 204). What the official yearbook does not tell us is that the "best known" status arose from a very public, transgressive relationship that was only very recently legalized (see *Loving v. Virginia*). Nor does it tell us the story of the verbal, physical, and extralegal harassment that the couple endured, as this young woman became embedded in a newly-emerging interracial family. Absent is the story of an early graduation, not to hide her premarital pregnancy, but to escape beatings in the girls' room. The notes left to both my parents in their respective books tell more of that story, a story that was one of mainly ties with whites lost, and ties with blacks gained.

My understanding of parenthood generally, and motherhood specifically, then, became one of simultaneous reward and sacrifice. While my mother lavished attention on me, and I was largely secure in the knowledge and experience of extended familial love, she was clear about what she gave up, in lost educational and work opportunities, in lost opportunities for a sense of self, separate from familial statuses of wife and mother. I am not always sure about how intentional her clarity was, but certainly over time I experienced her bond to me as one that was nearly suffocating—in giving so much to me, I was supposed to give myself back to her, be always on her side, be her first and best friend, take her with me always.

My mother's increasing lack of independent persona—or her resentment of my not getting on board with her interpretations of how deeply I should identify with her notion of my place as her daughter/best friend—was not something I saw developed in the othermothers in my life, although these were women whose lives emerged from far more constrained social circumstances, with far less egalitarian partners. My paternal grandmother, *Mama*, was one of fourteen children born in rural southern Arkansas. She married at fifteen to my then seventeen-year-old grandfather (one of eight children, born in northern Louisiana), and they were parents of the first of their ten children two years later. She had aspirations to be a nurse, but worked instead as a health care aid in a nursing home, (since she married when her educational opportunities were cut short by a teacher shortage at the "colored" school); her oldest son, instead, became a doctor. For my first three years, we lived in a house next door, and I was cared for, in part, by my aunts and uncles and grandparents. In contrast, my maternal grandmother, Grandma Cat (she had cats), was an only child who had lost her mother, and who was raised by aunts and uncles in addition to her father. She graduated from college, and married her then college sweetheart. They had six children, and although she had been a Journalism major who wrote during college, she would not work for pay until after her husband became too ill to do so, and she would not return to writing until she was in her sixties. She and her children also participated in raising me.

Through dominant social discourse and much theory I could be expected to ground my experience and development into mother-work nearly exclusively in the role models of the women I discussed above. However, since my exposure to theories of gender, race, class, and the family as both student and teacher, I have instead been guided to understand my motherhood as much in terms of the men in my life, and my relationships with them. Kathleen Gerson critiques the "vague and inconsistent" polysemics of mothering that encompass motivation, skills, behavior, and psychological states indistinguishably, instead arguing "that behavior, motivation, and skills are separate analytic categories that are related to each other in different ways, depending on the social context" (*Hard Choices* 33). As well, those behaviors, motivations, and skills are gendered through social contexts. Thus, *caring for an infant*, though a gender-neutral phrase with no inherent sex-linked traits or bona fide occupational qualifications, most easily, under the Standard North American Family ideology, becomes *mothering* rather than either *fathering* or *parenting*.

Although Talcott Parsons argued, "no other adult woman has a role remotely similar to that of the mother" (324), the concept of the othermother outlined by Collins is well established, as are its everyday lived experiences; in contrast, the concept of the "other father" is/are not (Lempert). While there have been increasing moves in both everyday discourse and policy towards an emphasis on the physical presence of fathers in direct caring roles and tasks, the most sweeping policy change aimed at poor Americans and their families once again maintained a primary focus of discursive and behavioral efforts at the breadwinning and biological role of fathers (Curran and Abrams). Curran and Abrams's investigation of the discourse of the 1996 *Personal Responsibility and Work Opportunity Reconciliation Act* (PRWORA) also examined the literature produced by state- and local-level social agencies that focused on "emotive paternal involvement" that "constitute[d] a contemporary 'hegemonic masculinity'" (670-671). This literature (and, indeed, the PRWORA itself) ignored scholarly literature that demonstrated the complex emotive, biological, and economic involvement poor men and men of color always have had to children (Curran and Abrams 668-670), and largely fed into reifying Father as singular and all-encompassing a role as Parsons laid out for Mother.

When I recall my own socialization, I find neither a world of emotive, nurturing women utterly distinct from economically responsible, emotionally distant men (the SNAF), nor one of strong women going it largely alone due to irresponsible men (the dysfunctional Black matriarchy of Moynihan's political mythology). My own very active mother was not unique as the one who fulfilled the variety of tasks that make up competent care for a child. As much Mother as she was to me, my experiences as the child of a distinct, particular mother were still fundamentally grounded in othermothering. However, it was as much the men in my life that were both competent othermothers, as well as "emotive" *and* "responsible" men, my father and my otherfathers. These men, unlike my diverse group of women othermothers, were overwhelmingly Black men: my father, my paternal grandfather, most of my uncles, particularly my father's older brother. These were the men who played with me, took me to work with them, taught me to read, taught me at least half of my cooking skills and love for food and gardening, as well as men who financially supported me, ranging from the normative breadwinning perspective, to Papa's pocket full of change given to his Ladybug, his first grandchild, to spend at the candy store, to the sharing of adult home space while I completed my education and began my professional career. It's these men I look to as I attempt to make my own mothering, because it is only through partnering with a supportive father for my children that I can actually achieve the sort of motherhood I think best for myself and my family.

VIGNETTE: OTHERMOTHERING, MOTHERWORK, AND SOCIAL MOTHERHOOD

Othermothering, as Collins has deployed the term, is about both showing up support for the daily motherwork that children need, as well as it is a social task, one not isolated to the imagined atomistic nuclear family unit as a variety of social actors deploy the SNAF. Again, my family socialized me into this way of thinking, and it isn't a way of thinking and arranging my life, my motherhood, that takes me either away from or towards domesticity, or my career, even as it is a way that pushes my husband towards being an "involved father". In the motherwork I do as a genealogist/family historian, I frequently look through family photos. In those images, I see evidence of that socialization. In the seemingly endless amount of photos I now have of my son, I see how I am deploying othermothering across the spaces where the motherwork of my family continues to play out. By consciously constructing myself as the hub-node of an othermothering network, the motherwork I manage is purposefully co-constructed co-parenting that must acknowledge an even broader range of participants than I think even the expansive concepts of othermother and otherfather have done, while at the same time not being a vague notion of the importance of the "village" it takes to raise children.

Photos of me with my father's younger siblings, and my mother's younger brother reflect my position within a familial web of care that, as an only child, socialized me to expect to care for children when my turn would come in a fundamentally different way than if I had just had my two parents as active caregivers.

These experiences left me with the indelible internalization that anyone within reach who is at all capable does what s/he can to provide the variety of tasks and resources that children need to live, even if s/he is also a child.

In demonstrating that these experiences were not just a tight-knit family, but a particular way of doing motherwork borne out of necessities of social location in a hierarchy, and individual choices of how to perform and inhabit racial and gender identities, we have to go beyond the boundaries of bloodmothers, blood kin, or even fictive kin (Collins *Black Feminist Thought* 119).

After having spent the first three years of my life living in a tiny duplex next door to the huge house (huge to me as I was a small child), of my paternal grandparents—far east of the racial dividing line of the city, with a large urban garden in the back yard—I moved with my parents to Columbia, MO, primarily for my father to complete his BA degree. Since both my parents worked and took classes, I spent the bulk of my daytime hours for the next couple of years at the Child Development Laboratory preschool at the state university. Thus, I went from one, albeit family-based, non-SNAF model of childcare directly into another. Again, neither my mother herself, nor women in general were, to me, default primary caregivers. Even though all the teachers I recall from preschool were women, because my mother worked outside the home at generally opposite times as my father, I spent equal amounts of time in one-on-one parenting contexts with each of them. This familial structure—full of co-parenting in all spheres, othermothering/fathering by extended family and non-kin in informal and formal settings, (both family friends and in curricular and extracurricular community settings),—carried me through my entire life as a dependent child, and currently flows on through my current motherwork.

I don't keep my son by my side in an attempt to make him into a satellite of Mother, His Whole World. I don't attempt to be all things to him not merely out of the necessity of keeping my full-time job (the salaries of two tenured professors, one of whom is a white man in a STEM field, provide a huge safety net for the vagaries of life), but because of my conviction regarding how to confront and live within an ongoing hierarchical structure that still says that my family as I define and live it doesn't meet the standard. Othermothering *is* necessary for me to meet the demands of my work schedule, and also necessary if my spouse and I want involved fatherhood; especially if we intend on raising another budding othermother/father. Structuring ways for men to both othermother, (i.e. incorporate here-to-fore markedly feminine ways of parenting and performing domestic labor), *and* otherfather, (i.e. expanding the responsibility of various forms of capital beyond one's own kin), could lead to an ideology of parenting that is child-focused in a way that does not simultaneously erase the self-hood and self-capacity of adults. While at the same time acknowledges, that these children are still someone else's children, who are still grounded in an ethic of caring for a network, and in turn receiving care themselves (Sarkisian and Gerstel; see also Laquer 159).

While we can discursively decouple the economic and nurturing spheres of being responsible for children from their gendered spheres fairly straightforwardly, it is of course the biological sphere of parenting where applying broad understandings of gender neutrality break down most easily. Simultaneously the starkest arena of the sexual division of labor; the actual sex-linked features of parenting—conception, gestation, labor/delivery, and breastfeeding—are not in fact the only biologically-linked features of childcare; even if they may be the most intimate. In addition, as bodily-grounded as they are, they are also, (and increasingly so), separable from the bodies of the various possible parents within whom they reside, and as easily commodified and exploited as any other alienable labor (see Laquer 156-157).

Similarly to Collins's deployment of motherwork, Thomas Laquer calls for "a labor theory of parenting in which emotional work counts" (155). His essay is focused on fatherhood, and tracing the history of the complicated physical and mental connections fathers have had to their children, he argues for exposing the nurturing that fathers have in fact always done. While Laquer highlights the reality within hegemonic ideologies North Americans have inherited, the visible, physically-connected parenting of gestation in particular has not always meant that therefore motherhood is in fact the more connected, important source of parenthood (158). Laquer's larger point is to argue that in human culture, "*is* does not imply *ought*,"

> the unproblematic nature of fact especially in relation to such deeply cultural designations as mother or father and to the rights, emotions, or duties that are associated with them. The "facts" of motherhood—and of fatherhood for that matter—are not "given" but come into being as science

> progresses and as the adversaries in political struggles select what they need from the vast, ever-growing storehouses of knowledge. (158)

I went through three experiences with the pregnancy that produced my son that threatened my health and life, and the health and life of my son. However, I can never even come close to telling those stories without talking about the ways in which they are a "labor theory" of fatherhood, of fatherwork, of husbandry in its now rarely-used sense of domestically centered productive and reproductive labor.

Being two academics grounded in social and physiological approaches to the body, my husband and I did a great deal of reading from abroad and deep group of expert and lay advice literature, all aimed at parenting practices. These practices that impact approaches to parenting range from how one is to prepare the body to successfully conceive, to what one is allowed to take into the body once pregnancy is achieved, and what is considered "best" to give a child. Nearly exclusively, this advice literature is still aimed at women and mothers. My husband became an involved manager of the things that made the physical labor of gestation easier for me. While this encompassed traditionally masculine care-taking tasks, such as heavy lifting (although my luggage-on-wheels was invaluable), it rapidly came to center on my husband's take over of the realm of food provision. At first it was making sure I had nausea-abating crackers by the bed, and taking over a lot of the meal preparation, but when I developed gestational diabetes, he put his physiological expertise and clinical experiences to work. He designed an Excel worksheet that tracked nutritional intake and blood sugar, so that it was easy to put together a meal that followed the guidelines the community health dietician and my OB gave us, and we could quickly figure out what affected my blood sugar. Using this tool custom-made by my spouse was a way of making food preparation easy for someone who only knew how to make a few dishes, and those few were decidedly not on the approved list for a diabetic. While he'd long been a fully equal cleaner and organizer of the domestic sphere, taking over the kitchen put him as husband and expectant father into the iconic heart of the home; he was the Angel of the Hearth.

Laquer distances himself from making his connection to fatherhood for several reasons. One, Laquer's understanding and connection to fatherhood as a practice is grounded in the idea of patriarchal ownership of having produced the child, through the highly valued labor of having conceived. In this sense, Laquer's conclusion ends up valuing idea over matter, mind over body, and of seeing insemination as the important engine and spark of life (158-159). At the same time, he circles back around to locating fatherhood in a physically/bodily-grounded experience of emotional labor,

> I write as the father of a daughter to whom I am bound by the 'facts' of a visceral love, not the molecular biology of reproduction. The fact of the matter is that from the instant the five-minute-old Hannah—a premature baby of 1,430 grams who was born by Caesarean section—grasped my finger ... I felt immensely powerful, and before the event, inconceivably strong bonds with her. Perhaps if practitioners of the various subspecialties of endocrinology had been present they might have measured surges of neurotransmitters and other hormones as strong as those that accompany parturition. But then what difference would that make-with what is one to feel if not with the body? (159)

Laquer describes his emotions in bodily terms—"visceral"—as well as making the factual point that emotions, in and of themselves, are the result of bodily chemicals. The emotionally laden care giving my husband had engaged in up to my thirty-first week of pregnancy was largely directed at me and not the fetus. He worried, as much about what having gestational diabetes would eventually mean for someone with my family history of Type II diabetes. When we discovered that the sudden lower abdominal pain and increasing fever that I was experiencing was not early labor, but both a severely enlarged gallbladder and a very likely burst appendix, his attentive labor became more parentally-directed. His concern was primarily on whether he would lose me in addition to the child that he'd felt move, but hadn't seen or touched.

We awaited my surgery. A surgery which might leave me with two fewer organs, a C-section, and a baby in the NICU, or might leave me, my child, or us both, dead. Chris remained calm and clinically observant, as I had to suffer through a replacement of my IV. Through the drug-induced dissociation I was already experiencing, I remember feeling sad, terrified, and yet resigned. Chris stroked my face and held my hand and said, "Everything will be alright. I'm not worried." I felt his distinctly clammy hands, knew he was trying to be brave and manage my fear and stress for me. I was drugged enough not to let him, and said, "Yes you are honey; your hands are totally clammy." I could literally feel his fear; feel how hard he was working to conceal his labor. This sort of physically palpable emotional labor didn't (and hasn't), stopped. Along with the care giving made necessary (but not hired out to another woman, such as a doula) by the cholorectomy/appendectomy and the emergency Caesarian section that occurred seven weeks later, the husband/father I share my household with, has made it so I would never refer to either of us as the primary parent. Such a person does not exist from our perspective, nor, we think, from our son's.

Even though I also engaged in the next most Bona Fide Occupational Qualification-laden of parenting tasks—breastfeeding—I accomplished that labor with the help of technology. We fed our son with my breast milk, but after his second week, we fed him from bottles after I pumped it from my breasts, and but for the stomach bug that laid us all out for nearly a week just before his first birthday, I would have continued past his first year. Although exclusively pumping includes most of the inconveniences of both breastfeeding directly (e.g., I had two bouts of mastitis) and formula feeding (lots of equipment to carry, and keep clean), it afforded my son with two primary parents. After our shared six weeks of FMLA leave was up (because we both work for the same employer, if we both wanted FMLA leave, we had to split the allotted twelve weeks), we alternated days working from home until our son entered part-time day care at six months of age.

I'm not a Total Mother (Wolf), and while there is some praise, as backhanded and awkward as it can sometimes be, for the mother who has secured the help of the father in doing what is presumed to be her job, more of that praise is lavished on the father for being a good helper, a good babysitter, letting Mommy have a day off. If the incomplete mother instead gets help doing her fundamental job from anyone other than family members and like-minded close friends, she is guilty of neglecting her duty, of not raising her own child, of not being a full-time mom.

While my son is not embedded in the same dense geographical family nest that I was, he still has as many othermothers and other-fathers as I did. His first preschool teacher made two collages and mounted poems that made the practice of othermothering explicit.

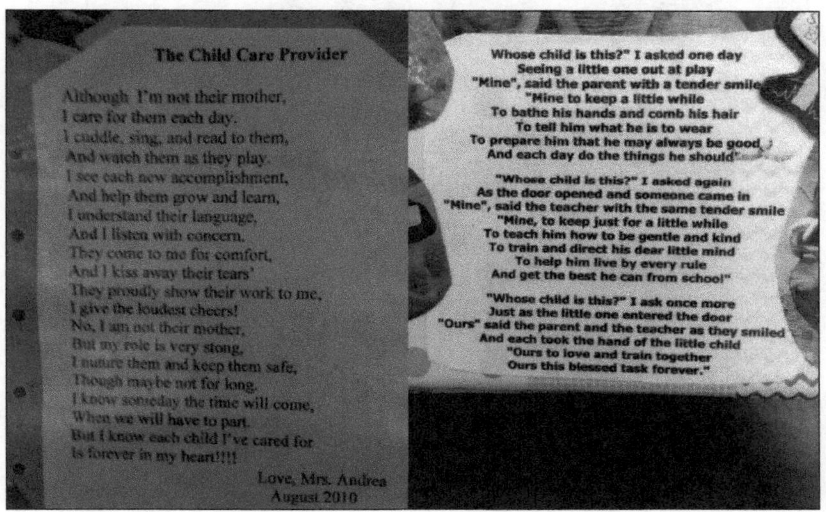

In writing about the permanence of othermothering that is made through adoption, Kathleen Silber and Phylis Speedlin argue,

> There are no first or second-best parents in this human experience. There are only adoptive parents who can never give their biological heritage or genetic future to their child and birthparents who cannot raise a child born to them. Both sets of parents in reality experience an incompleteness and loss. The child, in turn, can never be parented by *one set* of parents. He needs the adoptive set to provide the nurturing and shaping part of parenthood. He needs the biological set to provide the genetic past and future. (89)

Even as these authors try to equalize the parental members of the adoption triad, nurturing and shaping are not tasks that are, or need to be, delegated solely to parents. My son knows who his mother is, and in both my own experience, and from reports from others, he is quite secure in that knowledge, and attached to me. This does not prevent his attachment to others who perform every single task I have ever performed for him, save gestation and milk production.

VIGNETTE: MOTHERWORK AS SOCIAL LABOR

> As we looked at these colored women, late from Alabama, working in the Round-house in Cleveland, dressed in blue overalls with engineers' caps tipped back on their heads, perched on the side of a powerful locomotive while it rested from its journeying, we were reminded of Gulliver's Lilliputians playing about the great giant that had the power to crush them all ... and we asked ourselves what this adventure was that is calling women to take men's work in such strange places? Where will it end, what does it mean

> to women, to motherhood, to family life, and to that democracy that men are giving their lives for? (McDowell 3)

The words above come from Mary McDowell, a white labor and social activist from Chicago; hers words were mirrored by numerous reports, minutes, diaries, brochures, and other papers related to women's activism of the Progressive Era when I was expanding my undergraduate senior thesis work into a graduate second-year paper.[2] In particular, I was researching the ways in which white and black women responded to the issue of the densely packed cultural artifact of women's protective labor legislation.

Thomas Laquer states, "Feminism has been the most powerful denaturalizing theoretical force in my intellectual firmament" (157). Much like Laquer's intellectual genealogical debt to feminism generally, one particular arena of feminist agitation has been the foundation of my formal questioning of the naturalized social arrangements in which I am embedded. Protective labor legislation is important to the field of women's activist history, as with suffrage it is arguably the most prominent and successfully implemented political achievement of the women's movement. The intersections between powerfully constraining social categories, and the importance of understanding "the interplay of the race-class conflation with gender" in the "social perceptions of Black and white women's work roles" (Higgenbotham 259) are plainly visible throughout the discourse of and policies produced by the movement. As a social movement issue, labor policy for women melded "workers" and "women" and produced a revised image of the "working-woman." It merged—often paradoxically—middle-class notions of delicate ladies and socialist demands for dignified labor. This was a public discourse, a field, in which the hegemonic definition of "woman" was challenged and rearticulated. The outcome of this work was a changed discourse of womanhood that nevertheless retained much of what progressive political actors confronted when seeking to reform the conditions of womanhood.

Work as a concept carries with it a complex bundle of associations with other social fields. Public labor market work in general is masculine, while labor in the domestic arena in contrast is largely feminine. Further complex nuances modify these generalities, and particular kinds of market labor are, for example, historically linked to whiteness and working-class status, thus making industrial labor as well as *family* farming white man's work (e.g., Foner, 1995).[3] Other kinds of labor are associated with other social statuses, so that while domestic labor is feminine, paid domestic labor is poor, black, and female; working, Irish, and female; immigrant, poor, and Hispanic. Policy tended to reinforce cultural ideals, translating certain union demands for an eight-hour day for *workers* into state protection for *women* and *mothers* (Gatson "Labor Policy and the Social Meaning of Parenthood"). Research on the framing of the social problem of women's paid labor, and how best to facilitate and regulate it, has been formative for the ongoing framing I do for my own paid/unpaid labor, my own professional/familial identity work, which is all arguably motherwork.

Organizations like the ones McDowell belonged to supported "social legislation," which easily became part of the social responsibility and civic housekeeping duties that they claimed as their own (*Woman's City Club of Chicago 190-11 Yearbook*, 1911: 2; Woman's City Club *Bulletin,* January 1917: 3; March 1917: 5). McDowell's report on working conditions above represent motherwork that began as voluntary social work carried out by the daughter of a steel rolling mill owner that turned into the profession of social work as that field was established at the heart of the sociology/social work professional development arena of the University of Chicago.

Both of my parents worked in social service arenas (social work & community development/urban planning)—yet it's my mother's field of work that is labeled as an extension of the presumed nature of her womanhood—social work equals social mothering. The social services fields dominated by men (urban planning and community development) may be cast in terms of social *engineering* (gendered masculine by connotation) and/or as paternalism (denoted masculine) far more comfortably than what we generally understand to be "social work," the woman-dominated applied side to the man-dominated research side of "sociology" (however much the two actually overlap in practical terms). I now find myself, nearly twenty years after my first graduate school research experience and a professor in my own right, attempting to think through how—or if—it is appropriate to cast what I do for a living as motherwork in the larger social sense. As a woman of color and sociologist in academia, is my teaching othermothering and motherwork? Is my research? If it is, is it because I'm a woman, and now a mother, or are the tasks themselves just what Collins described, "'Work for the day to come'" accomplished across several terrains at once? The intellectual spaces I have long occupied are Alma Maters—mothers of the soul that could be spaces wherein I deploy mothering of the mind beyond my own child (Collins *Black Feminist Thought* 198, 211-212), placing the labor of ideation onto a social mother rather than a biological father (see Laquer 158-159). But the labor I engage in for pay—teaching, writing, and researching for and with students—covers the exact same set of tasks that my husband does across the same campus. If his parenting must be described in mothering terms, but his paid labor never is, are we persisting in making sex/gender-linked traits that are in fact not naturally so?

I began my research career grounded in two projects that carry motherhood at their core: interracial marriage and protective labor legislation. The first project was grounded in my own familial experiences, coming at them for the first time from a formal sociological perspective. The second, while on its face a more formal set of legal and social concepts, was also largely grounded in familial experiences: from my earliest memories, all the women in my family worked for pay outside the home, or expected to do so. Having been raised to self-identify as a feminist—my mother collected *Ms.* magazine's "Stories for Free Children" for me; as well, both parents encouraged me to read and discuss the magazine itself—learning the social history of political movements that affected my everyday life has been the core project of my intellectual development. While I certainly understood many of the ways my social position and ties affected my life chances, I was not so precocious as to recognize their complex nuances. As I've become a scholar and professor, I have struggled to teach standpoint theory as a knowledge-based autoethnographic approach to analyzing one's life as it is embedded in the social world even as I struggle to not let students slip into sloppy anecdata as they inappropriately generalize experiences and cultural tropes (see Tamas 261-262). At the core of that attempt is getting the students to critically ask, as Collins has demanded in her investigations of epistemology, "Where does my knowledge come from, and how is it deployed across the social landscape?"

I have written elsewhere of grounding this practical approach to sociology into my undergraduate courses (Gatson "Living, Breathing, Teaching Sociology"). One of the courses I teach regularly, and increasingly from an inquiry-based and writing intensive perspective, is marriage and family. I became a scholar of motherhood long before I became a mother, and I find that my own actual motherhood is a lived reality of navigating a variety of discourses of motherhood, scholarly and popular. I teach explicitly from a Black feminist/intersectional perspective that was deeply influenced by participating in the first Black feminist theory courses offered at my graduate institution, and being introduced to *Black Feminist Thought* therein. Over time, I have found it most useful to delineate the various tasks, identities, statuses/roles, and institutions that each of us actually do and inhabit, and are presumed to do, by virtue of our social location(s). The task arenas of parenting can be broadly broken up into three categories: economic, biologic, nurturing (Gatson "Labor Policy and the Social Meaning of Parenthood"). What goes into each of these categories is often straightforward and obvious, but just as often the content of the categories is culturally contested, and ever-shifting. While institutionalized and thus resistant to individualization, this content is simultaneously made up of the everyday decision-making of women and men, and all of those choice-points are more or less explicitly engaged with the hegemonic understandings of gendered, raced, classed, and sexualized selves.

CONCLUSION: INTERSECTIONALITY, AMORPHOUSNESS, SIMULTANEITY

As I now have to simultaneously sustain actual daily practice of motherhood, and scholarly and pedagogical engagement with motherhood as a theoretical concept, I find that historical and contemporary activism and advice literature targeting mothering, scholarship on mothering, pedagogy of mothering, and everyday practice have collided into a volatile stew that I then have to analyze, assign importance to, decide whether to incorporate into or discard from scholarship/ teaching/parenting, and repurpose in an ongoing bid to give my whole life meaning and utility. The vignettes herein represent some of that "stew" in an attempt to take advantage of evocative data points that, I hope, provide answers and open up further generative questions for both myself, and the reader. The vignettes loosely followed the matrix of parenting tasks (Ibid), and I aimed for an analysis of motherhood that is intersectional in both identity and action. This matrix is connected to both what one has to do for the self and what one has to do (or manage to have done) for those one mothers/parents—pay (Economic), act (Biologic), and care for (Nurturing).[4] Through developmental stages as we age, we each experience being enmeshed in this matrix, and over time we develop our own more or less culturally appropriate approaches to accomplishing all aspects of it.

Public discourse casts motherhood in terms of qualifiers and acronyms—Stay-at-home-mom (SAHM), Work-at-home-mom (WHAM), working mother, and my least-favorite, full-time mother. The rise of the term WHAM attempts to lessen the divisiveness of the mommy wars (look, it says, all women work, and all their work holds value), I see the deployment of the label 'full-time mother' go right along with the fairly thoughtless phrases "well, I want to raise my children myself" or "at least one parent should be raising the kids" written and spoken by many of my students as we discuss just how it is they think the tasks of family and parenting will and should play out in their own lives and across society. I say 'thoughtless,' because they've said it to me as I stood before them obviously pregnant, and they've said it to me as I stand before them teaching them for pay, while they know my son isn't right there in the classroom with us. While speaking the desire for a fulltime mother, they are clearly contrasting that set of tasks with an identity that they think I don't have. But how exactly is it that I am not always fully my child's mother? Do I still lay claim to Parsons's singular role? Yes, if that role is understood as an amorphous one, simultaneously engaged in motherwork, understanding the intersectional individual as one whose motherhood is "simultaneously socially developed and physically located in individual bodies and experiences and is thus both relational (in a genealogical and social sense) and experiential. This way of understanding [motherhood] alerts us to its fundamentally political character, rather than its merely physical character" (Gatson "On Being Amorphous" 27).

In many ways, motherhood is the frontline of everyday status politics, and as it is actively naturalized ideologically and institutionally, most of us can never do it quite right. Now, at the end of this essay, I am 43, with a completed home study and a four-year old itching to be a big brother. A four-year-old that still asks questions about "that baby that was too little to stay" (how he describes the miscarriage that he remembers). I now must confront my analytical parenting matrix in yet another personal realm. If our adoption is successful, it will be an open one, taking the networked parenting model I've lived through and deployed into new territory, becoming an adoptive family that "model[s] kinship as a life-long process of developing and sustaining networks of people who claim one another and share resources and care-giving" (Gailey 377). Of course, that's putting a rather shiny face on the adoption industry and its processes. In this realm, the child is still seen as a status resource. Adoption makes a parent, it flows from the biological labor of poorer people to people richer across multiple forms of capital, and the economic and nurturing resources flow largely if not exclusively to the adopted child, and rarely if ever back to the birth family. These are overwhelmingly one-shot, one-way deals. Having been through the biological labor field involved in motherhood, and continuing to get valuable social compensation for those labors, I am constantly thinking about biological motherhood and the biological tasks/labor/compensation (or lack thereof) involved in parenting. I am also thinking about the intertwined problematics of essentialization and bodily integrity, of essentializing motherhood with a connection to biology, without erasing the very embodied (raced, classed, gendered, and sexualized) fact of where any future child of mine is almost certainly going to come. It is highly unlikely to be from my body, but the ongoing physical and mental tasks of parenting would be grounded in me and my husband's physical and biological worlds.

The decoupling of mothering from the physical is essential to women being in the public world—at least in its current patriarchal and capitalistic hegemony. I've experienced the benefits of that decoupling first hand through both technology and othermothering/fathering. However, the control of women's bodies is an ongoing issue, as is the control/taking of their children. Although just about anyone could parent, not everyone is actually allowed to, and both historically and today, that has not nearly always been primarily about who is doing an objectively outright awful and harmful job at it (see Gordon; Coontz). As much as the control of the reproductive labor of women has been a central feminist concern, how is the control of the reproductive labor of men similarly problematic? Is the physical separation of men from fathering tasks—either in a traditional economic provider sense, fraught concerns for birth fathers (too many rights or not enough?), or in the prison-industrial complex where poor fathers and fathers of color are completely severed from their children—bad for both mothering and fathering?

Joan Wolf has argued that in what she calls the current risk-averse society, Total Motherhood is put forth as the solution to society's ills, and that "representations of biological practices reflect unequal distributions of power" (xiv). Adoption, like breastfeeding, involves intensive biological labor, but it violates the moral code of Total Motherhood, especially if it is open adoption, where one admits from the outset and always that she didn't do all the work, and didn't "optimize" her child's environment, and will never thus be SNAF-approved. Can we though argue for an active redefinition of this concept—a concept that takes the whole intersectional person, the amorphous identities deployed across social contexts and vis-à-vis other people (Gatson "On Being Amorphous") into consideration when defining motherhood, rather than seeking to have the person subsumed into a totalizing, ideal concept of motherhood, as well as defining it as the actual set of resources every child needs/is entitled to? Can we make "mothering" and "fathering" into "parenting," de-gendering it, without simultaneously erasing the bodies doing the work? Can parenting become a form of alienable labor that is paid through networked reciprocity that expands the pathways of social capital as well as literal capital? So much of inequality is structured through the family (Mueller), but how much can we dismantle at the micro-level? How much does my motherwork—from the everyday parenting tasks to this very essay—even matter?

Note: *All photographs are part of the author's personal collection.*

[1]As a formal theoretical statement, Black feminist theory has many antecedents. In this case, I would highlight the work of Dubois wherein he put forth the concepts of "double-consciousness" and "the veil." In one of the earliest formal statements of the theory, Deborah King references this work, expanding it into the concept of "multiple jeopardy, multiple consciousness." See also Davis; Hall; and Higgenbotham; and nineteenth-century sources such as Wells-Barnett; and *A History of the Club Movement Among the Colored Women of the United States of America.*

[2]In the Northwestern University Sociology Department at the time of my attendance, we did not have a thesis option connected to the Master of Arts program, but rather a second-year paper as part of the Ph.D. program requirements. This paper functioned largely like a master's level thesis.

[3]Although rural labor has historically been linked to blackness, the family dimensions of Black farming have long been significantly downplayed.

[4]Here, the "act" of the biologic category encompasses both physical action and thoughts—I do not seek to reify a mind/body dichotomy, given that thoughts are produced, and feelings are experienced, grounded in the chemical and electric environment of our brains, which are as "meaty" as our bodies.

WORKS CITED

A History of the Club Movement Among the Colored Women of the United States of America, As Contained in the Minutes of the Conventions, Held in Boston, July 29, 30, 31, 1895 and of the National Federation of Afro-American Women, held in Washington, DC, *July 20-22, 1896.* Pamphlet, 1902, Chicago Historical Society.

Collins, Patricia Hill. *Black Feminist Thought.* 1990. New York: Routledge, 2000.

Collins, Patricia Hill. "Shifting the Center: Race, Class, and Feminist Theorizing about Motherhood." *Mothering: Ideology, Experience, and Agency.* Eds. Evelyn Nakano Glenn, Grace Chang, and Linda Rennie Forcey. New York: Routledge, 1994. 45-65.

Coontz, Stephanie. *The Way We Never Were: American Families and the Nostalgia Trap*. New York: Basic Books, 1992.

Curran, Laura and Laura S. Abrams. "Making Men into Dads: Fatherhood, the State, and Welfare Reform." *Gender & Society* 14.5 (2000): 662-678.

Crusader, Yearbook of Southes at High School, Kansas City, Missouri. 1969.

Davis, Angela Y. *Women, Race, and Class.* New York: Vintage, 1983.

DuBois, W. E. B. *The Souls of Black Folk.* New York: Signet, 1982 (1903).

Foner, Eric. *Free Soil, Free Labor, Free Men: The Ideology of the Republican Party Before the Civil War.* Oxford: Oxford University Press, 1995.

Gailey, Christine Ward. "Adoptive Families in the United States." *Families and Society.* Ed. Scott Coltrane. Belmont: Wadsworth, 2004. 377-389.

Gatson, Sarah N. "Labor Policy and the Social Meaning of Parenthood." *Law and Social Inquiry* 22.2 (1997): 277-310.

Gatson, Sarah N. "On Being Amorphous: Autoethnography, Genealogy, and a Multiracial Identity." *Qualitative Inquiry* 9.1 (2003): 20-48.

Gatson, Sarah N. "The Genealogy of Daisy Bates, Version 8.0." *Qualitative Inquiry* 11.2 (2005): 291-295.

Gatson, Sarah N. "Living, Breathing, Teaching Sociology: Using the Micro to Illuminate the Macro." *Faculty of Color Teaching in Predominantly White Institutions.* Ed. Christine Stanley. Bolton: Anker, 2006. 153-165.

Gatson, Sarah N. "Self-Naming Practices on the Internet: Identity, Authenticity, and Community." *Cultural Studies ←→ Critical Methodologies* 11.3 (2011): 224-235.

Gerson, Kathleen. *Hard Choices: How Women Decide About*

Work, Career, and Motherhood. Berkeley: University of California Press, 1985.

Gerson, Kathleen. *No Man's Land.* New York: Basic Books, 1993.

Gordon, Linda. *Heroes of Their Own Lives: The Politics and History of Family Violence.* 1988. Urbana: University of Illinois Press, 2002.

Hall, Jacquelyn Dowd. "'The Mind That Burns in Each Body': Women, Rape, and Racial Violence." *Powers of Desire: The Politics of Sexuality.* Eds. Ann Snitow, Christine Stansell, and Sharon Thompson. New York: Monthly Review Press, 1983. 329-349.

Haraway, Donna J. *Simians, Cyborgs, and Women: The Reinvention of Nature.* New York: Routledge, 1991.

Higgenbotham, Evelyn Brooks. "African-American Women's History and the Metalanguage of Race." *Signs: Journal of Women in Culture and Society* 18.2 (1992): 259-274.

King, Deborah K. "Multiple Jeopardy, Multiple Consciousness." *Black Women in America: Social Science Perspectives.* Eds. Micheline R. Malson, Elisabeth Mudimbe-Boyi, Jean F. O'Barr, and Mary Wyer. Chicago: University of Chicago Press, 1988. 265-296.

Laquer, Thomas. "The Facts of Fatherhood." *Rethinking the Family: Some Feminist Questions.* Eds. Barrie Thorne and Marilyn Yalon. Boston: Northeastern University Press, 1992. 155-175.

Lempert, Lora Bex. "Other Fathers: An Alternative Perspective on African American Community Caring." *The Black Family: Essays and Studies.* Ed. Robert Staples. Toronto: Wadsworth, 1999. 189-201.

Loving v. Virginia, 388 U.S. 1 (1967).

McDowell, Mary. "Opportunity?" Typescript, November 1, 1917. Mary McDowell Papers, Box 3, Folder 15. Chicago Historical Society.

Mueller, Jennifer C. "Tracing Family, Teaching Race: Critical Race Pedagogy in the Millennial Sociology Classroom." *Teaching Sociology.* 31 July 2012. Web. Accessed Sept. 18, 2013.

Narayan, Kirin. "Participant Observation." *Women Writing Culture.* Eds. Ruth Behar and Deborah Gordon. Berkeley: University of California Press, 1995. 33-48.

Parsons, Talcott. "Sex Roles in the American Kinship System." *Social Theory: The Multicultural & Classic Readings*. Ed. Charles Lemert. Boulder: Westview, 1993 (1954). 324-328.

Sarkisian, Natalia and Naomi Gerstel. "Kin support among Blacks and Whites." *American Sociological Review* 69.6 (2004): 812-837.

Silber, Kathleen, and Phylis Speedlin. *Dear Birthmother: Thank You for Our Baby*. Dallas: Corona, 1991.

Smith, Dorothy. "The Standard North American Family: SNAF as an Ideological Code." *Journal of Family Issues* 14.1 (1993): 50-65.

Sperling, Susan. "Baboons with Briefcases vs. Langurs in Lipstick: Feminism and Functionalism in Primate Studies." *Gender at the Crossroads of Knowledge: Feminist Anthropology in the Post-modern Era*. Ed. Micaela di Leonardo. Berkeley: University of California Press, 1991. 204-234.

Tamas, Sophie. "Autoethnography, Ethics, and Making Your Baby Cry." *Cultural Studies ↔ Critical Methodologies* 11.3 (2011): 258-264.

Wells-Barnett, Ida B. *Selected Works of Ida B. Wells-Barnett*. Compiled and with an Introduction by Trudier Harris. New York: Oxford University Press, 1991.

Wolf, Joan B. *Is Breast Best? Taking on the Breastfeeding Experts and the New High Stakes Motherhood*. New York: New York University Press, 2011.

Papers of the Women's City Club of Chicago. University of Illinois, Chicago Circle, Department of Special Collections.

Patricia Hill Collins as Pedagogical Mother

ABIGAIL L. PALKO

IN A RECENT RETROSPECTIVE assessment of her work-to-date, Patricia Hill Collins writes of the multiple identities that people have ascribed to her,

> I am all of these things some of the time, but none of these things all of the time. The fluid nature of how others view me as well as how I see them has shaped the content and process of my intellectual production. My work encapsulates multiple situated standpoints—distinctive, competing, and often contradictory angles of vision that shift not only when I vary physical and intellectual social locations but also when times change around me. While it has been tempting to simplify my situated standpoints and merge them into a homogenous narrative to make the world more comfortable for me, my challenge has been to sustain a commitment to dialogical knowledge production, especially in situations of conflict. (Collins "Looking Back" 14-5)

While Collins is reflecting here on her work as a whole with a focus on "scholarship in service to social justice," as she terms it, this observation encapsulates her specific contribution to motherhood studies, as the simple substitution of "maternal" for "intellectual" reveals (Collins "Looking Back" 14). She asserts that two core questions anchor her scholarship: "What accounts for social injustice? What can we do to foster social justice?" (Collins "Looking Back" 20). I offer here a brief reflection on my own use of Collins' work in my classroom in the hope that it will help to illuminate the emancipatory potential of her scholarship with regards to feminism and more specifically, motherhood studies.[1]

Patricia Hill Collins' extended theorization of African American mothering practices stands among the most important and influential of her many intellectual contributions to black feminist studies. In addition to this, Collins' theoretical application of intersectionality to analyses of motherhood as an institution and as a practice has also introduced new paradigms of understanding to motherhood studies. It is precisely this articulation of the intersectionality of the lived experience which makes Collins' work so pedagogically valuable. I have taught Patricia Hill Collins' work in a variety of courses, from a first-year "Introduction to Gender Studies," to a senior-level (fourth year) elective, to a graduate-level (doctoral) seminar on motherhood studies entitled "Mother Nature? An Introduction to Motherhood Studies."[2] Her theorization of intersectionality, explication of stereotypes of black femininity, and valorization of Other Mothering as maternal work have provided my students with an introduction to important forms of feminism not previously encountered by many of them. For those students whose life experiences had already familiarized them with these concepts in a practical manner, experiencing them in an academic setting usually proves transformative, once they realize that our work isn't just going to focus on white middle/upper class issues.

THE ENVIRONMENT

I teach at a private, Catholic, research-oriented university. Our undergraduate population totals approximately 8,500 students, 48 percent of whom are female and 52 percent are male. Students of color comprise 22 percent of the undergraduate student population. An accepted perception of our students is that they come from privileged backgrounds (although not all do); nevertheless (or because of it), they are firmly committed to the ideals of Catholic social justice teaching, and 80 percent of them engage in some form of voluntary service-learning during their undergraduate career, either in the local community or on service learning trips during our semester breaks. But while our students might work with mothers like those embodied in and empowered by Collins' work, the reality of their personal history is often quite different. One student bravely admitted, "I honestly have been so sheltered (despite public high school experience) that I have never given much thought to differences and stereotypes about black women" (Intro). And despite our institutional commitment to diversity and social justice, our students have expressed a sense that we do not actually discuss these issues in an effective enough manner. As one undergraduate told me, "I feel that because of the lack of diversity of this campus, black societal issues and in general racial societal issues are not as often addressed both academically and socially as they should be" (Intro). Another student explained that the prevailing attitude she has encountered in her years has been an assumption that "if they [black people] work hard than they will no longer be disadvantaged or stereotyped" (Intro); her implication was that the majority of her peers do not understand the impact of intersecting oppressions on the realities of people's lived experiences. Collins' work is thus a crucial pedagogical tool for me, which I use as a point of entry for my students into an important conversation.

When I consider my students specifically in the context of motherhood studies, I am struck by the marked difference between their experiences of mothering and my own, that is, the mothering practices they were exposed to in their formative years, the media portrayals of these practices, and their sense of what maternal identity they will assume in the future. They are the after-product of the environment described by Susan Douglas and Meredith Michaels in *The Mommy Myth* (whereas I grew up in this environment). They have inherited a media-shaped, culturally significant ideology, their childhood influenced by their mothers' embrace, (or alternately, their rejection) of the mothering practices characteristic of the new momism that Douglas and Michaels define as:

> the insistence that no woman is truly complete or fulfilled unless she has kids, that women remain the best primary caretakers of children, and that to be a remotely decent mother, a woman has to devote her entire physical, psychological, emotional, and intellectual being, 24/7, to her

> children.... The "new momism" is a set of ideals, norms, and practices, most frequently and powerfully represented in the media, that seem on the surface to celebrate motherhood, but which in reality promulgate standards of perfections that are beyond your reach. (4-5)

Born in the early- to mid-1990s, many of my students were raised by stay-at-home mothers, and many envision a similar future for themselves. Beneficiaries of this ideological media onslaught (characterized by Douglas and Michaels as a war against mothers), they have been trained to believe in its worth, which is not to imply that they have all unquestioningly and/or willingly adopted it. But they are also simultaneously largely unknowing inheritors—they did not directly experience the cultural phenomena analyzed by Douglas and Michaels. Rather, their exposure to media images of American mothers is better encapsulated by car commercials—think of the Subaru commercials, featuring the hockey mom driving to the Pogues' song "If I Should Fall From Grace With God"—and TV moms of the 2000s like Lois from *Malcolm in the Middle*, Marge of *The Simpsons*, or Lorelei from *Gilmore Girls*.[3] Even the political usage of maternal images analyzed by Marsha Marotta, who notes that the label "Soccer moms" was "used seriously and yet for the most part not taken seriously—the same impossible position mothers face when American politics and culture claim that motherhood is the most important role for women yet offer more support to corporations and other countries than to mothers" predates today's college undergraduates' childhoods (329).

Students such as mine are the conflicted legatees of the paradox that Shari L. Thurer observes in *The Myths of Motherhood: How Culture Reinvents the Good Mother*[4]:

> But there is no getting around the fact that ambition is not a maternal trait. Motherhood and ambition are still largely seen as opposing forces. More strongly expressed, a lack of ambition—or a professed lack of ambition, a sacrificial willingness to set personal ambition aside—is still the virtuous proof of good mothering. For many women, perhaps

> most, motherhood versus personal ambition represents the heart of the feminine dilemma. (287)

This final claim—the balancing of motherhood and personal ambition against each other as the "heart of the feminine dilemma" for most women—is questionable at best, and Collins' work helps us articulate its problematic nature, as I hope my discussion of my students' responses to reading and discussing her work will demonstrate. My students, though, will most likely enter the maternal conversation through the door marked "The Mommy Wars." And for those who do, their lives will coexist alongside those of women who enter into the maternal public sphere through other doors, including mothers of color, nonmothers, and Other Mothers. And the successful navigation of the maternal waters on the part of all of this upcoming generation of women depends on mutual understanding. Their experiences are, as Douglas and Michaels argue, intimately intertwined:

> Although it may have been hard to recognize at the time, the war against welfare mothers was indeed part of the broader war against all mothers. For momism to work as a new norm, there had to be delinquents who dramatized what happened to those who failed to comply, delinquents other mothers could feel comfortable about putting in detention. (177)

Consequently, for many of my students, my primary pedagogical aim in introducing them to Patricia Hill Collins' work is to initiate the contact that social scientists argue leads to a deeper understanding of the impact of intersecting oppressions on other women's lives and mothering practices. Such understanding will hopefully then lead to a more effective political engagement, as Marotta suggests, thereby creating the kind of cross-racial solidarity that bell hooks has advocated as necessary for "any revolutionary change, any transformation, individually or collectively" (Marotta 334; hooks 410). In fact, Collins has offered a richly developed philosophy of pedagogy that has the power to guide our efforts in nurturing the growth of motherhood studies; in her essay

"On Our Own Terms: Self-Defined Standpoints and Curriculum Transformation," Collins concludes, "Placing African-American women and other historically marginalized groups in the center of analysis opens up possibilities for new constructs, paradigms, and epistemological approaches to knowledge" (381). Throughout her analysis in this essay, she asserts the revolutionary potential created by viewing black women's mothering through their own standpoint lens.

TEACHING COLLINS

The challenges faced by maternal scholars reflect (and reinforce) an institutionalized marginalization of mothering, and we would do well in our reformatory efforts to remember Collins' assessment that "while knowledge representing elite group interests supports systems of domination, the self-defined knowledge created by men of color, women, gays and lesbians, students, and other subordinated groups can provide a powerful tool in challenging those same systems" (Collins "On Our Own Terms" 367-8). In my own teaching, I have consciously worked to embody Collins' approach. She advocates:

> Instead of trying to incorporate scholarship on historically marginalized groups into existing curriculum phases, an alternative approach to curriculum transformation might begin with efforts to describe and interpret the self-defined standpoints of women of color, racial/ethnic groups, and other subordinated groups whose self-defined standpoints have been essential to their survival within interlocking structures of race, class, and gender domination. (Collins "On Our Own Terms" 370)

Thus, when I teach Introduction to Gender Studies, I use "Mammies, Matriarchs, and Other Controlling Images," a chapter from Collins' ground-breaking *Black Feminist Thought*.[5] This reading is one of a dozen in the opening unit, "Constructing Gender/Constructions of Gender," and it is one of four that deal with constructions of femininity. I present Collins' theory of intersectionality before we discuss Collins' explication of the controlling images of Black femininity. I teach it in conjunction with Andrea Shaw's work on body size, a pairing that gives the students language to talk about body image issues and to start to parse out differences in racial expectations for beauty. For many of the students in this introductory course, this is their first academic exposure to these ideas. They can recognize that they have been exposed to these stereotypes, but they do not have the scholarly language to analyze them. This encounter is potentially painful for them; as one of my graduate students explained in her rationale for including Collins in a freshman English course on the African American Presence that she is designing,[6] "I see this material being controversial and, hopefully, uncomfortable for the students. I think through discomfort we can truly learn to uncover the issues at hand and truly grow in how we articulate our opinions" (McDermott). As she explains, the ways of thinking about and defining the female body and perspective that Collins offers are new for many students, regardless of racial identity, and they push students toward intellectual honesty and development. I have seen this growth in my own course.

When I taught the chapter in the fall of 2012, one of my teaching assistants (a graduate student) observed that the students deeply engaged with the material. They questioned whether these controlling images were still salient in our culture, and they echoed the double standard enmeshed in controlling images of white and black motherhood, asking, "Why are white women who raise children alone praised for being 'strong', while black and Latina women who raise children alone are as stigmatized and chastised for 'scaring their men away'?" This is an insightful comment; as my teaching assistant noted, "Given the demographic of undergraduates at this particular university and the make-up of this particular course being mostly white, upper-middle class, I am convinced it is particularly important for these students to be exposed to black feminist thought and social analysis from the perspective of a so-called cultural 'other'" (Simpson). I surveyed this group of students before and after reading Collins' chapter[7] from *Black Feminist Thought*. Prior to reading the chapter, my students contended that the most prevalent stereotypes in U.S.

society today about black women include, but are not limited to: loud, obnoxious, not well-spoken, welfare queen/mother, angry, overweight, "more tough/maybe masculine (know how to protect themselves)", lazy, uneducated, helpless, objects of black males, the Mammy, lacking any power, good athletes and singers, sassy, promiscuous, opinionated, and intimidating (Intro). One student's answer encapsulates the overall tenor of the students' collective responses: "Where I grew up, people always described black women as being loud, drama queens, divas, always fighting. Black women stereotypically have big behinds and can dance really well" (Intro). When questioned about stereotypes of black women specifically as mothers, the responses were more diverse. One referenced Michelle Obama as a positive role model; one described the images presented in Tyler Perry movies; and a third described the matriarch, and she was careful to note that this is a positive image (Intro). The vast majority, though, expressed a variation of this comment: "They are portrayed as poor mothers who do not provide for their children" (Intro). Without realizing it, they articulated the crucial elements of the controlling images dissected by Collins, setting the stage perfectly for our discussion. Pedagogical goals for this day included an analysis of Collin's methodology in the chapter, explication of the controlling images that Collins analyzes, and a discussion of the impact of these images. When I surveyed the students after the class about the impact of the reading, their insights confirmed my decision to teach this piece. One student wrote, "I feel as if she clarified stereotypes I was already aware of yet didn't realize... as if I had already so associated black women a particular way in my mind that I subconsciously knew/recognized what she was talking about, without knowing the proper jargon" (Intro).

In an interdisciplinary graduate-level course that I designed and taught, and which served to function as an Introduction to Motherhood Studies class, it was paramount that the students explore a variety of maternal identities and issues, so we devoted a week to African American engagements with motherhood studies. I included readings from several prominent black theorists, including Collins' pieces "Shifting the Center: Race, Class, and Feminist Theorizing About Motherhood" and "The Meaning of Motherhood in Black Culture and Black Mother-Daughter

Relationships, " Dorothy Roberts' "Killing the Black Body" (all reprinted in *Maternal Theory*), as well as Angela Davis' "Racism, Birth Control and Reproductive Rights" (from *Women, Race, and Class*), Alice Walker's "Everyday Use" and "One Child of One's Own: A Meaningful Digression Within the Work(s)," and Laurie A. Wilkie's conclusion to *The Archaeology of Mothering*. This session strove to meet Collins' pedagogical challenge: "By presenting Black mothers, for example, as empowered figures within the constraints of race, class, and gender oppression, Black feminist analyses embrace an alternative construct of motherhood" (Collins "On Our Own Terms" 372). For many of my graduate students, like my undergraduate students, Collins' discussion of Black mothers was their first encounter with a self-defined perspective of a role that they had mostly encountered through media distortions. Reading her work had the immediate impact of confirming their collective intellectual hunch that the diversity of mothering practices demands attention from multiple disciplines and standpoints. One secondary benefit for them, though, is that Collins' refusal of a patriarchally-defined, institutional motherhood frees them to reconceive motherhood in general through a different lens. Easily seeing the value of Collins' theorizations for their own work, these students all intend to incorporate readings from her in their own future syllabi.

ACCEPTING HER LEGACY

Collins' pedagogical reflections serve as an important model for those of us who wish to integrate her work into our courses.[8] She interrogates African American studies, asking, "is [African American studies] offering alternative models analyzing contemporary race, class and gender oppression that will empower African American women and men?" (Collins "It's In Our Hands" 130). When I teach literature electives, especially when they are cross-listed with our Africana Studies department, I include her most relevant (to our novels) essay or chapter in the theoretical readings, usually her work on Other Mothers, and model an analytical application of her work to literary readings for the students. These efforts are rewarded as they push the students to richer readings: "New concepts, paradigms, and epistemologies emerge from this process when multiple standpoints are investigated" (Collins "On Our Own Terms" 371). Regardless of the course, the students respond well to this new (to them) voice. One student in my introduction course concluded her pre-reading survey with a wistful observation that "I wish I had both more opportunity to learn about these issues and to interact with black women; just studying the literature will not provide real understanding" (Intro). She is completely correct.

"Mammies, Matriarchs, and Other Controlling Images" functions to initiate the contact students crave—not to replace it. Collins' insistence that these controlling images of black women "transmit clear messages about the proper links among female sexuality, fertility, and Black women's roles in the political economy" (Collins 90) opens up several valuable avenues of exploration for us: first and foremost, the students are given the scholarly language to articulate the stereotypes that they have encountered (and probably not known how to question) and to deconstruct them. In the deconstruction of these images, they begin to explore the structural connections between race and idealizations of the "Good Mother," the economic factors undergirding women's mothering practices, and the public interest in the (as they assume) private practice of reproduction. It is my pedagogical goal for them to understand that, as Laura Harrison argues in her analysis of cross-racial gestational surrogacy, "The creation of a family is defined by one's ability to produce children, which is a reflection of the power of the nation, and therefore vulnerable to state intervention. If childbearing increases the strength of the nation and is a reflection of it, then certain people will be encouraged to reproduce over others" (270). In the larger feminist project, her work also offers a crucial insight, as a former graduate student articulates: "Collins is invaluable, because she helps us as teachers and students to redefine feminism as being this inclusive idea, but also by challenging the definition as it fits for white women, and allowing us to see feminism as this distinct entity for black women and their experience" (McDermott). This student plans to teach Collins in the upcoming semester at an institution similar to mine, noting that, "For my predominantly affluent, white students, I believe that Collins will expand their minds to include the black feminist perspective, and to see the political in the black female body in a way that they may not have been challenged to do so before" (McDermott). Another student, pursuing a graduate degree in sociology, articulates how Collins' work is pedagogically appealing: "her application is less esoteric and theoretical. Students will be able to identify racism, gendered prejudice, classism, etc. and see how they all come together as intersectionality. Students will be able to see that –isms rarely stand alone but are a combination of race, class, gender, and sexuality—as demonstrated by Collins" (Sun). As a result of both the clarity of her theory and her prose, Collins challenges my students in a non-threatening (but definitely challenging to previously held beliefs) way. As my TA mentioned in a follow-up,

> *What struck me most about their discussion was that they managed to discuss and challenge Collins in respectful ways, despite not having any black women representatives in the room. In other words, they did not take the overwhelming absence of black women in their classroom as license to reject Collins' claims or argument. While this might be a marker of their cultural sensitivity or even their maturity, I rather took it as an indication of Collins' effectiveness as a writer and intellectual to radically complicate students' ways of thinking.* (Simpson)

For my students, reading Collins provokes an influential paradigm-shift in thought. I have found that highlighting Collins' work in the graduate course has inspired these future professors to consider using her work themselves. An important element of my pedagogical engagement with Collins is thus its contribution to the training of graduate students; sharing Collins with them brings her work to the next generation (this is important, as Elizabeth Higginbotham notes in her essay in the symposia on the contributions of Collins in the February 2012 issue of *Gender & Society*, 23). They seem to find this intellectual task an inspiring challenge: "The students ... raised thoughtful questions, responded to each other in respectful ways, and even considered some of their own experiences in light of this new information/way of thinking about the female experience. I hope for a similar experience in teaching this to my future classes" (Simpson).

They rightly view her as an important model for the intellectual work of theorizing difference. As one notes, Collins articulated for academia the connections among –isms that already shaped people's lived realities. It was through honoring her personal experiences that Collins developed one of the most significant sociological theories for modernity. This radically alters the academic approach: "The theory of intersectionality is able to capture real life situations without being dissociated by claiming that –isms are standalones in society" (Sun). Another explains its power in similar terms:

> *Besides offering a much better way of understanding systems of oppression than the additive model that people often imagine, her thinking offers a great model for what it means to conceptualize a new paradigm. I've found that students are often great at coming up with answers to specific questions but sometimes struggle to understand how to effectively challenge the terms of a question or system. So, I like what her work offers epistemologically for students as well as what it offers in terms of content.* (Hughes)

In turn, I have found their enthusiastic embrace of Collins—coupled with the immediate understandings of her significance demonstrated by my undergraduates—an inspiration to my own pedagogical and scholarly work, particularly when the wide view of social oppressions is considered. These experiences confirm for me the intrinsic value of offering students scholarly endorsements of nonhegemonic mothering practices.

Pedagogically speaking, Patricia Hill Collins' work offers a wealth of resources for the university professor seeking to recognize his/her students' realities and/or expand their perspectives. Many of the students in my Introduction course expressed sentiments similar to this one: "The reading had me asking a lot more questions about how much stereotypes are affecting our society" (Intro). I also surveyed students currently taking a literature elective with me to determine the lasting impact of exposure to Collins' work.[9] In this course, there are 17 students; nine of them are majors or minors in the gender studies program, and if they have taken our introduction course, they have read Collins' work. Sadly, none of the non-majors/non-minors had read anything by Collins (though some of them had heard of her). Of the nine gender studies students, two were new to the program and have not yet taken the Introduction course. The other seven were able to respond to my survey.[10] Even those who articulated a sense of not remembering Collins' work clearly (about half of them) retained enough of a sense of her work and its import to discuss the ways it opened them up to seeing gendered and racialized stereotypes, so that six of the seven answered the question "How did this reading shape your thinking?" with a variation of "greater focus on stereotypes in my every day. More focus on gender stereotypes with regards to other cultures or races" (GS Students). Certainly, getting these responses from students who had read the work over a year earlier and who were provided with no notice that I'd be asking the questions (I distributed the survey in the last 15 minutes of class one day with no prior notice; the students were told that while they could put their name on them, I was looking for anonymous responses and I did not include a space to record their names) was very heartening—this is the kind of positive follow-up feedback educators rarely receive at any level! One former student, who read "Black Women and Motherhood" last year for the Introduction course, described Collins' impact as "ma[king] me consider motherhood from a perspective I hadn't thought of before"; this student further clarified, "It made me consider how much more nuanced privilege is than simply patriarchy over women" (GS Students). In other words, these readings are introducing my students into a conversation that they might have sensed was happening, but one that they did not directly experience prior to our class.

Any list of theorists who have made foundational contributions to the field of motherhood studies must include Adrienne Rich, for her distinction between motherhood as institution and motherhood as practice; Sara Ruddick, for her conceptualization of maternal thinking and her articulation of preservation, nurturance, and social training as its goals; and Patricia Hill Collins, for the added depth provided by her theorization of the oppressive power of intersecting identities on Black women's mothering practices. But furthermore, when I consider the impact her work has had on maternal scholars, I see the ways that she herself has fulfilled Ruddick's commission for us, her academic daughters. She has provided us with the tools necessary to fully apply the work of Rich and Ruddick, she has given us the language to express a multitude of realities—she has nurtured and trained us, schooling us in rigorous, intellectually honest research methodology. As another former student wrote, "A lot of what she said surprised me and was the first time I really thought about different types of mothering and how race changes/inscribes mothering" (GS Students); Collins has empowered me to open my students' eyes to realities they have not yet experienced. For the students of color in my courses, the experience is valuable in several ways. The first is that her work confers academic legitimacy on their experiences by placing them in the privileged subject of knowledge position, and secondly, it provides a scholarly space to explore these experiences. As one former student expressed it, "Reading Collins as a black female made me understand more fully the complex discrimination experienced by black women" (GS Students). This, for me, is the ultimate imprimatur of academic relevance and excellence: in reading Collins, students see themselves (and their relation to the women whom society has labelled other than them) with new clarity, and it is through this process that Collins is a pedagogical mother of all of us working in feminist and motherhood studies.

[1]I would like to thank my students whose astute and empathetic responses to Patricia Hill Collins' work over the years has inspired me, especially those who took the time to so thoughtfully answer my questions for this essay.

[2]All syllabi referenced in this essay are available at www.abigail-palko.net.

[3]Interestingly, though, for them, the TV mom is no longer a highly salient influence. When I asked them which TV moms they remembered from their childhood, one student answered, "I don't—it's a blank when I try to think of an answer," and more than half of them emphatically concurred with her.

[4]In Thurer's otherwise excellent survey of the Good Mother, the image is silently very white. This very whiteness, of course, reflects the dominant cultural belief that race is a predicative factor of successful mothering.

[5]In the past, I have used the chapter "Black Women and Motherhood" from *Black Feminist Thought*; while I find this chapter hugely informative for my own scholarship, I have come to see how "Mammies, Matriarchs, and Other Controlling Images" better fills a lacuna in my students' understanding of multiple oppressions. I also once tried the more recent essay "Prison for our Bodies, Closets for Our Minds: Racism, Heterosexism, and Black Sexuality," but it proved a little too inaccessible for students just being introduced to gender issues and questions of intersectionality. I have also successfully used her essay "Toward a New Vision: Race, Class, and Gender as Categories of Analysis and Connection."

[6]For this project, I interviewed four former graduate students via email, each of whom has agreed to be identified by name. I am deeply grateful for their contributions to this essay.

[7]The survey was administered in person in class, and while students were told they could identify themselves, anonymity was encouraged as the default by the omission of a specific place to write down their names. The students were given the surveys before we read the Collins chapter and they returned them after our discussion of the reading. Of the 20 students in the class, 12 of them chose to submit it. References to these surveys will be indicated as (Intro).

The pre-reading survey included the following questions:

- What stereotypes are prevalent in U.S. society about black women?
- What media images/portrayals of black women as sexual beings do we have?
- As mothers?
- Have you read anything academic about black women's position in American society? Studied racial issues in a previous class?
- Is this something we do or do not discuss here?
- Is there anything else you'd like to add?

The post-reading survey asked:

- How has Collins changed/nuanced your understanding about the stereotypes that are prevalent in U.S. society about black women?
- How might you use her to challenge a stereotype?
- How did this reading shape your thinking?
- Is there anything else you'd like to add?

[8]See, for example, "It's in Our Hands: Breaking the Silence on Gender in African American Studies" and "The Emerging Theory and Pedagogy of Black Women's Studies."

[9]References to these surveys will be indicated as (GS Students).

[10]The questions on the survey were:

- What Collins piece(s) have you read?
- How well do you remember them?
- Do you remember your initial impression of her work?
- How has Collins changed/nuanced your understanding about the stereotypes that are prevalent in US society about black women?
- How might you use her to challenge a stereotype?
- How did this reading shape your thinking?
- Is there anything else you'd like to add?

WORKS CITED

Collins, Patricia Hill. *Black Feminist Thought: Knowledge, Consciousness, and the Politics of Empowerment.* 2nd ed. New York: Routledge, 2000.

Collins, Patricia Hill. "The Emerging Theory and Pedagogy of Black Women's Studies." *Feminist Issues* 6.1 (1986): 3-17.

Collins, Patricia Hill. "It's in Our Hands: Breaking the Silence on Gender in African American Studies." *Understanding Curriculum as Radical Text: Representations of Identity and Difference in Education.* Ed. Louis J. Castenell, Jr. and William F. Pinar. Albany: State University of New York Press, 1993. 127-41.

Collins, Patricia Hill. "Looking Back, Moving Ahead: Scholarship in Service to Social Justice." *Gender & Society* 26.1 (February 2012): 14-22.

Collins, Patricia Hill. "On Our Own Terms: Self-Defined Standpoints and Curriculum Transformation." *NWSA Journal* 3.3 (Autumn 1991): 367-81. Web. 12 October 2012.

Collins, Patricia Hill. "Prison for Our Bodies, Closets for Our Minds: Racism, Heterosexism, and Black Sexuality." *Sex, Gender, and Sexuality: The New Basics: An Anthology.* Eds. Abby L. Ferber, Kimberly Holcomb, and Tre Wentling. New York: Oxford University Press, 2009. 115-35.

Collins, Patricia Hill. "Shifting the Center: Race, Class, and Feminist Theorizing About Motherhood." *Mothering: Ideology, Experience, and Agency.* Ed. Evelyn Nakano Glenn, Grace Chang, and Linda Rennie Forcey. New York: Routledge, 1994. 45-65.

Douglas, Susan J. and Meredith M. Michaels. *The Mommy Myth: The Idealization of Motherhood and How It Has Undermined All Women.* New York: Free Press, 2004.

"Gender Studies Students Survey." Survey. 5 September 2012.

Harrison, Laura. "Brown Bodies, White Eggs: The Politics of Cross-racial Gestational Surrogacy." *21st Century Motherhood: Experience, Identity, Policy, Agency*. Ed. Andrea O'Reilly. New York: Columbia University Press, 2010. 261-75.

Higginbotham, Elizabeth. "Reflections on the Early Contributions of Patricia Hill Collins." *Gender & Society* 26.1 (February 2012): 23-7.

hooks, bell. "Sisterhood: Political Solidarity between Women." *Dangerous Liaisons: Gender, Nation, and Postcolonial Perspectives*. Ed. Anne McClintock, Aamir Mufti, and Ella Shohat. Minneapolis: University of Minneapolis Press, 1997. 396-411.

Hughes, Jessica. Personal interview. 27 August 2012.

"Introduction to Gender Studies." Survey. 29 August 2012 and 31 August 2012.

Marotta, Marsha. "Political Labeling of Mothers: An Obstacle to Equality in Politics." *21st Century Motherhood: Experience, Identity, Policy, Agency.* Ed. Andrea O'Reilly. New York: Columbia University Press, 2010. 324-37.

McDermott, Courtney. Personal interview. 24 August 2012.

O'Reilly, Andrea. Ed. *Maternal Theory: Essential Readings*. Toronto: Demeter Press, 2007.

Shaw, Andrea. *The Embodiment of Disobedience: Fat Black Women's Unruly Political Bodies*. Lanham, MD: Lexington Press, 2006.

Simpson, Meagan. Personal interview. 8 September 2012.
Sun, June. Personal interview. 28 November 2012.
Thurer, Shari L. *The Myths of Motherhood: How Culture Reinvents the Good Mother.* New York: Penguin, 1994.

Mothering Past the Line of No Defense

Millennial Daughters on the Path to Crafting a Black Feminism of Their Own

TONI C. KING AND S. ALEASE FERGUSON

GENERATION X,[1] followed by those dubbed the millennials,[2] and subsequently new millennials[3] are far less likely to have a well-formulated understanding of how race, class, and gender operate in daily life. They are even less likely to have a handle on the subtle dynamics of modern days isms (e.g. racism, classism, sexism) that operate covertly, yet produce outcomes that continue to marginalize overtly (Higginbotham 4-14; Ogletree 6-13). These young women's lives, generational and psychological distance from the U.S. Civil Rights and Feminists Movements, and the differentially connective and depersonalizing effects of technology make them less likely to be equipped to respond strategically to the incursion of modern day "isms" into their personal experiences. This is especially the case when these women find themselves at predominately white academic institutions. Even though young Black college women of today often arrive on our campuses with a strong desire to give back to their communities, as well as to achieve personal success, many have had limited exposure to the critical knowledge base transmitted within stage appropriate Motherline tutelage. Patricia Hill Collins termed this traditional form of woman-to-woman cultural transmission "mothering the mind."[4,5] Mothering the Mind includes wisdom that elder women, community mothers, and mother centered networks use to give practical help and emotional support as a political strategy for waging resistance to oppression, and to apply healing modes for individual and collective survival.

In addition to the limitations on their comprehension of the matrices of oppression, a decline in access to a robust and multi-faceted web of othermothers affects numerous black girls in route to womanhood. This is true, ironically, even among those who reside among what W. E. B. Dubois[6] (33, 75) referred to as the talented tenth. For it is among our college matriculated women that we have had an opportunity to see the gaps in Daughterline learning and preparation to carry out their own aspirations for leadership praxis and social uplift.

In light of this socio-political landscape our college-aged women enter the ivory tower with distinctive personal and socio-political vulnerabilities. When it comes to "mothering the mind," this group demonstrates a disconnected schema of knowledge relative to their age and stage of early adult development. The gaps in their exposure to and internalization of the "curricular" process and content of mothering the mind, erodes and complicates their own agendas for practicing leadership. Commonly compromised is the tactical knowledge of racial uplift and, the skills for engaging in development through constructive relationships with self and others. Those girls who sense the missing connections of support and apprenticeship to a tradition of black feminist/womanist leadership, eagerly and persistently seek out black feminist other-mothers, who are also educators, in their college communities. As co-authors, we are among the black feminist othermothers, who are also educators, which these young African American female millennials reach out to. Although they initially struggle to articulate what they are in need of, we bond with them. Overtime it becomes clear that they see the needs for a mothering of the mind from the Motherline. We have heard this need expressed through such earnest comments as: "I just need that time with you," or "We don't even have to talk—you can talk and I'll listen," or "When can I have some one-on-one time? I know you're busy so even just twenty minutes will do!"

Beyond the desire for intimate connection accompanied by the desire to "sit at the feet of the elders," some women express a need for the psycho-spiritual experience of being "schooled, tutored, apprenticed, mentored, healed, and held" within the Motherline circle. This group realizes the potency of such unions, and that connection to one such mother is always a connection to the circle of women past, present and future. At a tangible level they seek our knowledge, feedback, socio-political commentary, the testimony of our self-affirmation, ability to deconstruct the matrix of oppression and its manifestation in the lives of black women, especially as it is manifesting in their lives as women of color in the academy. Our experiences tell us that it is imperative for black woman feminist educators to understand the needs of current generations of black women, particularly those seeking a mothering of the mind. Yet, before we can develop pedagogical methods and epistemological stances that match the Motherline curriculum to the needs of the millennial Daughterline, we need to articulate what distinguishes current day mother work from past mother work. How is it different from what has historically been done to transmit the knowledge of cultural preservation and uplift? Collin's seminal work *Black Feminist Thought: Knowledge, Consciousness, and the Politics of Empowerment* is critically important to helping us understand "whether new, culturally specific, resilient lifelines must be created to ensure collective survival" (177).

To more sharply articulate contemporary issues in mothering the mind, we draw upon Collins' thematic framework that posits five themes within the traditions of mothering among African descended people, which embody cultural socialization from mothers to daughters. These core themes include: 1) the existence of bloodmothers, othermothers and women-centered networks; 2) Mothers, daughters, and socialization for survival; 3) Community Othermothers and Political Activism; 4) Motherhood as a Symbol of Power; and 5) The View from the Inside: Personal Meaning of Motherhood. We explore the first three questions from a five-fold thematic trajectory, to query the issues we see among our young women who seek the Motherline in academia. We approach our research from our own subjective experiences as a professor and administrator at a private, predominately white, liberal arts college (Toni King); and as, a professor for a proprietary,[7] predominately white university in a suburban setting, and social services administrator (S. Alease Ferguson). While our motherwork in its most general sense spans all genders, this essay focuses specifically on the African Diasporan Daughterline. Armed with Collins' considerable study of the meaning and issues of mothering and mother-daughter relationships we, methodologically, create an inter-subjective space in this essay by weaving Collins' work into our own study of black mother-daughter relationships.

Utilizing the first three overarching questions of Collins' framework, we, first, look into contemporary issues of mothering the mind. Second, we illustrate what we see as the most pressing issues among young women who seek out our feminist mothering. Third, we articulate our pedagogical and developmental interventions, across the Motherline to provide the Daughterline with connections to appropriate mother/othermother circles of care. Finally, we share some concluding thoughts or directions for further inquiry into this work.

WHENCE THE MOTHERLINE: COLLINS' THREE THEMES

We begin with Collins' first theme in *Black Feminist Thought,* "what of the existence of bloodmothers, othermothers and women centered networks?" as a bridge to discuss the presence of black women within the academy over the last two decades. There has been a tremendous reduction of accessibility to women who play the roles of othermothers and of women who serve such a role in a socially organized and cohesive manner. According to womanist scholar Stephanie Evans, among faculty, African American and women of color make up only two percent of the twenty-first century academy's demographic base in the U.S. As such, their very presence, contributions, and communal orientations are often marginalized in a mainstream academic environment. In such environments, individual achievement and competition are lauded over more communal orientations where helping the group succeed is of paramount value (135-136).

In a campus climate where othermothers are few, many girls come to us reminiscing about these cherished bonds. They speak of a caring teacher, a mentor, a role model or an aunt who has impacted their lives and worldviews. These women discuss their families and various communities in which the women are bonded to each other, offering instrumental and social support for one another; particularly when it comes to the communal rearing of children. Yet, over the past decade we have seen a drastic decrease in students who come from these communities of women. Fewer still describe being held securely within a community of neighborhood women, church women, rural /small town/ urban burrow women, who shared the responsibility for parental discipline, socialization to "lady-hood" or lady-like behavior, singling out for apprenticeship tasks that signaled to girls their own worth and leadership potential, etc. (Ferguson and King 167-69).

We encounter far more girls who have had to serve as supports; emotionally and sometimes financially, with their own mothers. At the same time, these same girls have excelled academically, managed to sustain their own sexual identity development in constructive ways, and are destined for making a name for themselves; by often times serving as a role model for younger siblings and fulfilling their bloodmother's dreams for their success. However, their needs for an ongoing mother-connection, and the craving for deeper levels of socialization from the Motherline are vast. For example, Alaycia, a student we interviewed about daily motherwork illustrates this very phenomenon. She dubbed me "Mother-King," (which I allowed her to call me after her own discernment about when and how to call me that), and told me her story in my office after having taken two courses with me and with us knowing each other for about a year. She explained first, why she had come to call me "Mother-King."[8] Her story was one of being a survivor within a family system beset by poverty induced stressors, parental substance abuse and early parental abandonment and loss. She was ultimately raised by her grandmother, and as a first generation college student—her beloved grandmother and remaining familial circle knew nothing of her struggles as a college student. These life experiences left her with a mother-hunger, and a need for a mothering of the mind that related to her future aims.[9]

Alaycia is not alone in her mother-hunger, which becomes acute in predominately white college settings where women of color face such extreme disconfirmation. They experience intense feelings that they can't go home again; folks back home berating them for losing "their blackness" because of their educations; etc. The contemporary mother-line no longer has the kinds of multiplex links that carry a full store of benefits. One in which women who nurture girls, are themselves inter-connected to a rich circle of women re-enforcing the lessons, gifts, pragmatic assistance, abundance, and messages of worth and affirmation for each other. Among our millennial daughter leadership aspirants, we hear them query the kinds of things they wish to work through with their mothers and othermothers that they feel they have not had sufficient time and conditions to explore. Since the turn of the twenty-first century, we have heard with growing intensity, appeals from our women students that replicate Alaycia's overall need for a Motherline bond. These appeals span themes for mentoring with respect to: spirituality vs. religiosity, healthy and constructive male female relationships, presentation of self in the dominant culture while balancing the need for cultural expression, cultivation of one's own beauty aesthetic, the socio-politics of Black woman-to-white woman relationships, crafting and negotiating personally and culturally congruent leadership—to name a few. All of our interviews reflect an escalation in the strength of the needs girls bring to us today. We now have students who have fewer women encircling them, and who have received less from the women of their various circles, because these women too are embattled from negotiating the modern day toll of intersectional oppression.

HOW DO WE SING A MOTHERLINE SONG IN A STRANGE LAND?

Patricia Hill Collins' second theme in *Black Feminist Thought* asserts that Black mothers engage in socialization for survival with respect to their daughters and otherdaughters. Utilizing Collins' "standpoint theory," we interrogate the extent of socialization needed by our black female college students with whom we negotiate othermother relationships. Collins defines "standpoint theory," as a shared perspective that black women have based on their common experiences of being black women in society. Key to Collins' definition of standpoint—is the role of institutionalized power. She writes: "An oppressed group's experiences may put its members in a position to see things differently, but their lack of control over the ideological apparatuses of society makes expressing a self-defined standpoint more difficult.... Groups unequal in power are correspondingly unequal in their ability to make their standpoint known to themselves and others" (26).

In this work, we further articulate a black women's standpoint as it is shaped in the context of faculty other mother-daughter relationships. The following questions serve as the methodological springboard for this articulation. What is the content of the socialization that black college women who seek personal achievement and leadership receive en route to womanhood? Where are the gaps in this socialization, and how does this affect their coming of age as leading women? What critical knowledge would invigorate their leadership, and prepare them to more emphatically seize places of leadership on the world stage? How do we meet them where they are, and engage in stage appropriate dispensation of socialization? To what extent have these young women experienced the motherly protection needed as they are taught how to negotiate their lives as black women? Lastly, we have to ask, what do daughter-line millennials know of the history of black women's leadership and how can we afford them opportunities to gain this knowledge when so many are averse to Black Studies and and/or Women's Studies where such information abounds?

Beyond simply having knowledge of the contributions of Black women to the racial project of liberation within the landscape of intra-American civil and human right, there is a need for young Black women to also be able to situate the contributions of their womanly lineage within a feminist/womanist tradition over time. Without this methodological feature of situating one's self within a larger narrative of one's feminist Motherline, these young women risk a loss of strategic alliances, diminished possibilities for coalition building, and truncation of within and cross race relational synergy in their leadership endeavors. Who will teach them how to survive the sexual politics of intersecting oppressions while rejecting and transcending these same power relations?"(275).

In our work as community and university othermothers, we see a decline in the knowledge of identifying and negotiating race, class, and gender relations among millennial daughters. Like many millennials (Thielfoldt and Scheef 135), they doubt the pervasiveness and perniciousness of systemic oppression in everyday life and interactions. While some are intellectually aware of some of the overt discriminatory practices, (such as racial profiling, disproportionate race based sentencing and incarceration, representations of blacks in the media and other macrocosmic manifestations of race), many know little of the daily subtleties of race-class-gender exhibited in the power relations of daily experience. Hence they find the cumulative effects of the micro-aggressions they experience in their daily lives at a predominately white college campus at times baffling, overwhelming, shocking and even traumatizing. Their feelings of indignation are evident in such statements as: I'm shocked that people feel that way about blacks in this day and age; I can't believe that a professor would say things that stereotype black people; or, my professors said nothing in class when outrageous statements were made about food deserts being a myth and that black people "don't want to work to purchase healthy and nutritious foods." More significantly, we observe them to be more impacted by the outcomes of these negotiations, less able to interrogate the racialized issues they encounter, to process them effectively with peers, to create strategic responses and action plans, and to heal in the aftermath with sense of self restored. For our black women students, limited socio-political readiness translates to a compromised ability to take up the reins of leadership, which is informed by a feminist politic of their choosing. It is this gap in knowledge that is of paramount importance to us. This is particularly evident, when it comes to the following case—Bryn.

Bryn arrived at the predominately white college of one of the co-authors as a vibrant, outgoing first year student who was identified early on as highly motivated, capable, assertive, and proactive in her approach to college life. By her sophomore year, Bryn was selected to serve in the coveted position of interviewer for the admissions office of the college. The role also included services as a tour guide for parents and prospective students, and occasional travel with the college's recruitment team. As a member of a team of students, Bryn was assigned to co-lead her team with a white female student of the same class rank. She immediately began to experience subtle challenges to her authority from her co-leader. For example, meetings called at times she could not attend, and her co-leader's forging ahead with preparations that should have been made collaboratively. In time, the co-leader filed complaints with the admissions professionals stating that Bryn lacked diligence, and the ability to carry her share of the workload, was difficult to reach via e-mail, and was not resourceful as a contributing co-leader. Bryn's credibility had been so undermined with the team and professional staff that she began to act out. As she put it, "I had a few choice words" with the co-leaders which sent that young white woman in tears to their supervisor.

When the supervisor made efforts to either refute or corroborate the co-leaders' allegations of Bryn's "lack of fit" for the position, others on the team also expressed discomfort with Bryn's communication style stating that it made them uncomfortable. Alternatively, when Bryn was silent so as to prevent "giving a few choice words," in response to behaviors from her co-leader that she felt undermined her role, her peers saw the silence as indifference. Soon after uncovering these dynamics the supervisor offered Bryn the choices of being demoted to a regular team member role, or to work under her co-leader's supervision, or to resign. Hurt and unable to grasp the unfolding of events, she chose to assume the "secondary" role of co-leader. Ultimately, feelings of outrage, and loss of faith in her ability to contribute to the team, led to lowered efficacy (e.g. missing meetings, delayed responses to co-leader requests). Shortly, thereafter she was terminated from the post.

By the time Bryn reached out for othermother assistance, she was quite depressed. Although able to keep up with her studies, she felt maligned. Once the rumor mill among her peers churned out the details of her being let go, the story took on a life of its own—making her feel more powerless. I found that in our newly minted mentor-mentee relationship, much work was needed in helping to deconstruct and re-frame the story in ways that were healing, affirming of her agency, and that would effectively situate the narrative within the context of white capitalist patriarchal supremacy and its effects on white female-black female relations.

In our conversations, when I asked whether, and how race or racism played a role in this series of incidents, she responded with honesty and fervent assertion:" I don't see anything in this story relating to race." After a great deal of reflective-oriented dialogue, she began to see the race, class, and gender implications. In these sessions we wrestled with her resistance to seeing racialized dynamics and implications. It became apparent that denial and blindness to racist dynamics was linked to her perception that the mere acknowledgement of racism reflected some form of victimology and degradation. Her tendency to locate all of her experience within her own faults and lack of knowledge was indicative of the limits of prior Motherline socialization and the transmission of tools for personal and collective survival. In our view, it was the power relations framework that Bryn had little practice examining, applying and using for her own restorative benefit. A good biblio-therapeutic resource for improving a student's understanding can be found in Patricia J. Williams' *Seeing a Color-Blind Future: The Paradox of Race.*

The kind of Mothering the Mind discussed in Bryn's case is more likely to have been filled when there was a connected community of black women available to girls and young women in their formative years. For someone of Bryn's generation to have missed age appropriate degrees of this training across their lifespans makes it much harder to begin to knit once she or others of her generation arrive at early womanhood. Ostensibly, their entire worldview has to make room for a new angle of vision—as Hill Collins would refer to it, a black woman's standpoint (225). However, this standpoint would be shaped by the particulars of their generational exodus from childhood into adult female status.

MOTHERING PAST THE LINE OF NO DEFENSE

The third theme in Collins' *Black Feminist Thought* is Community Othermothers and Political Activism, prior to the millennials' era, asserts that more black girls had direct exposure to the political activism of community mothers. While they may not have had a theoretical framework within which to position their experiential knowledge, they commonly had the "aha!" moments in our Black Studies and women's studies classes that they had indeed witnessed community other mothers in action.[10] Whether through embracing the Motherline imagination of their othermothers and role models, or through them pushing away intergenerational self-destructive behaviors of their immediate forbears, many want to bring their educations to bear in helping their communities face both the contemporary socio-cultural ills and socio-economic crises of our times. They want to engage in community activism and many avidly pursue service learning opportunities, volunteerism, and what the academy encourages under the auspices of civic education as well as opportunities to develop tools for sustaining and demonstrating respect within and across differences.

In spite of this desire for activism, today's young black undergraduate college women often reject feminism with little knowledge of how it might be critical to their leadership agendas. Many know little to nothing of the rich tradition of black feminist activists and intellectuals who gave leadership and service to society. Most have no knowledge that many of the "race women" of the 1800s and 1900s who had an agenda for black nationhood that framed women's issues as integral to the progress of the race just as it framed racial progress as integral to the successful evolution of the nation.

Specific limits to the leadership motility and potency of our college-aged women arise from this void in the mothering of their minds. Such limits include, but are not confined to

- Severely limited opportunities for cross generation bonding with women leaders who portray a complex view of the role and value of feminism including Black women's contributions to it.
- Reduced socialization and tutelage from the Motherline about the subtleties of working across the matrices of race, class, and gender to address pan-humanist agendas from a feminist vantage point.
- Limited dialogue with the Motherline that penetrates their learned reactions to the idea of "feminism" and that introduces interrelated feminisms such as womanism, black feminism, multicultural feminism, queer feminism, Mujerista feminism, etc.
- Subverted sister bonding and connections with black women peers who claim a feminist identity or feminist stance. This produces attributions and sets these relationships

up for ruptured expectations in which those who do not identify with the contributions of feminism perceive their black feminist sisters as having a wayward, or white-identified approach to social change that detracts from black in-group solidarity.

•Re-inscribed male defined roles for women in which issues affecting women's lives have no place in the work of resisting oppression by framing race not merely as the *primary* axis of oppression, but as the *only* axis of oppression. When women's issues are addressed, they are "policed" so that critiques of black male power and privilege are subordinated, and feminist perspectives are placed outside the sphere of legitimate discourse.

The barriers to this passing of the baton from feminist mothers and othermothers to daughters creates a dynamic of "no defense" with respect to the issues that college aged women face. At a time in their lives when they have finally arrived at young adulthood despite the dangers to them as Black women, there is a rupture in their ability to internalize a clear vision of how to become a leader and how that leadership will benefit from a consciousness of women's issues globally.

This thwarting of girls' sensitivity to women's issues on a local and global scale—a kind of woman-centered blindness—is of immense concern to us as feminist othermother educators. On campus, we see such "blindness" in the gender politics of Greek life, the sexual politics of black men and women on our college campuses, the failure to see the need to support Black women peers, faculty or staff via behaviors that run the gamut of benign disrespect, micro-assaults, or open hostility, the non-participation in woman-centered student organizations across race, and the inconsistent valuing of women in the context of woman-centered organizations within race (e.g. betrayals of sister-bonds, cruel gossip, hazing, unmitigated competition, entrenched enviousness), and many other manifestations of injured gender consciousness. We do not intend to frame all of the ways that socio-cultural conditions undermine an ethic of care and reproduce capitalist and materialistic orientations among youth. Yet, we acknowledge the larger social tapestry and the macro-cosmic factors impinging on black communities and youth of all socio-economic strata to embrace materialism and an epistemology of "I'm gonna get mine."

Fortunately, not all of the black women we encounter are in absentia at the table of feminism. Out of this cauldron of conditions that mitigate the spirit of activism among today's black women, we are highly encouraged by the fact that we still find so many young women who do wish to step up as leading women activists engaged in social and political uplift. Among the women we othermother, there are two pronounced patterns of participation in the feminist project: 1) the transgressive/insider and 2) the culturally resonant insider. Both patterns reflect the contradictory position of the Black woman millennial feminist and thus require us to position ourselves to support their constructions of their feminist political work. Examples of these two patterns of participation follow:

Teraya is an avowed feminist seeking a place of leadership viability on the college campus of one of the co-authors of this work. She is a senior who has worked diligently to negotiate spaces within the spheres of black community, white community and broadly defined women of color community. She expresses themes of distress in navigating her leadership as a black woman on who owns her feminist identity. These themes include: being perceived as having access to approval and favor by whites, being too non-traditional and engaged in activities that are "not black" (e.g. participation on the crew team, her major in marine biology, her membership in the student feminist group on campus), her membership in the Black Student Union while simultaneously speaking loving critique regarding clique favoritism among its leadership.[11]

Teraya's struggle to be accepted by the Black campus community for her feminist identity is further exacerbated by the life stage needs of her women peers regarding male female power relations. In the late teens and early adulthood, it is critical for Black girls and women to begin to clarify the daily dynamics of gendered relations (Ladner 110-112; hooks 160-162). It is key to be affirmed by black men during these gender identity development years to avoid faltering publicly in ways that get one labeled and constructed outside of what is deemed normal for a Black girl/woman. The intensity of the peer pressure to avoid "transgressing" the normal when it comes to embracing feminism, parallels that exerted on those who are pressured to avoid "acting white"[12] (Spencer and Harpalani 7). As long as feminism is seen only as "a white woman's thing," Teraya's feminism and cross-race alliances with campus feminists make her suspect among her black peers.

Barbara Smith's essay, "Introduction to Home Girls: A Black Feminist Anthology," in the cannon of womanist literature specifies the social constructions that obstruct Black women's embrace of feminism. These myths include: Black women are already liberated, racism is the primary or sole oppression for Black women, feminism is man hating, and women's issues are apolitical (xxxiii-xlvii). Black women who come to College with a readiness to explore feminism, or even more rare, those who come as avowed feminists, have typically had—some sensitization to gender issues through key mother figures who gave tutelage in the tradition of black feminist thought. Such girls had a feminist "mother of the mind" (Barkley Brown 88-89) or feminist political mother (Collins *Black Feminist Thought* 189) during their formative stages of leadership development.

Teraya's feminist praxis comes from her understanding of feminist thought. She was the beneficiary of a biological mother and othermothers invested in transmission of Motherline tutelage for political activism. Our purpose in the othermothering of women like Teraya is to make sure that they have somewhere to turn for social support, rejuvenation of flagging energies, deconstruction of in-group micro-assaults, and political strategizing across cultural communities within the college context. Key to Teraya's survival and flourishing is ongoing sense-making of what it means to be the transgressive insider who pushes the cultural boundaries by openly embracing feminist work among her Black peers. Motherline work needs to be continuously attuned to the transgressive insider's activities within the college leadership sphere—so that this young woman feels that the Motherline has her back.

A second example of political activism among our black women students is one that moves from the position of cultural insider and works deeply from what is already culturally resonant within

Black culture. Maya exemplifies the culturally resonant insider's pattern that we see among current day Black women students. Maya utilizes the cultural template of sisterhood connection that is accepted grounds for political and cultural work among black community life in the college sphere. The tensions she faces as an activist arise from the multiple corrosive conditions that attack black female bonding capacities. Themes from her experiences include: healing from an abusive male/female relationship in her college years, experiencing deep depression and low self-esteem that motivated her to compete with other women for male attention, becoming isolated from peer-woman-centered bonds. Her recovery and transformation in the context of an othermother connection gave her key support to seek professional counseling, work with faculty to earn extra credit to improve her grades, find her voice through creative writing and blogging, and ultimately build a leadership praxis by establishing a support group for women of color on the campus.[13] Although Maya did weave her college commitments into political activism, she was conscious of the reality that forging constructive sister bonds does not always raise consciousness of feminist issues. On the other hand, she did not feel as compromised as Teraya with respect to having a legitimized identity among her black peers on campus.

For our otherdaughters who are in the process of laying claim to Black feminist/womanist dimensions of their leadership, we find that they need our presence and abilities to help them theorize the issues they are encountering to leverage their own feminist praxis. What many of these highly motivated, well-educated black women are often missing, is a critical black feminism that frames their multiplicative identities, gives them ways of articulating their "race-gender" work, and provides them with a stance for responding to the false claim that they are endangering in-group political solidarity. Our political work with this generation of women requires the co-creation of a kitchen table that responds to their needs.

In conclusion, we reaffirm our cognizance of the shifts in access to the trifold conditions Collins posited as foundational to black girl-to-woman capacities for stepping into leadership within family, community, and society. Those cultural conditions include access to bloodmothers, othermothers and women centered networks, socialization for survival, and direct and long-term exposure to community othermothers and political activism. In this age of modern day racism made more insidious by its covert manifestations within the matrix of oppression, we see the institutionalized corruption of the tri-fold cultural curriculum Collins so aptly framed. We write this piece to illustrate how the academy can be one site for restoration from the gynocidal injury and loss incurred when systemic rupture to mothering the mind occurs among women of the talented tenth.

In this essay, we step out of the shadows of the ivory tower to point out the potential crisis of feminist leadership that we are particularly situated to correct. As womanist academicians, our work in the academy responds to the broader College community and remains pan humanist in scope. Nevertheless, within the spirit of a both/and epistemology we are also intentional in our woman-centered agenda to assist and develop women of color and Diasporan Black women's capacities to take their rightful place as feminist leaders. This agenda is a matter of ensuring the cultural survival of a people. It seeks to respond with potency to those millennial women who want to step up to their own feminist praxis and exert leadership in the world. Barbara Omolade is credited for describing the processes of othermother leadership development with the rising generation of women and girls as "the tradition that has no name" (see Belenky, Bond and Weinstock 11-12). When these daughters seeking to apprentice themselves to this tradition make overtures of need for othermother connectedness and tutelage, we assess and respond to the stage appropriate developmental needs they exhibit for leadership development.

First and foremost we make our presence available and construct relationships that carry the kitchen table into the hallowed halls of academe. By crafting vehicles appropriate to the context of the predominately white spheres of higher education (e.g. classes, seminars, conferences, fieldwork, community and civic engagement), we make spaces that are alive with dialogue and where black women can construct and deconstruct lived experiences that promote continued self-definition and the forming of their own standpoints. Second, we offer academic home places whether through our pedagogies, co-curricular opportunities (e.g. guest speakers, artists in residence, community activists, seminars, workshops, support groups, dialogue sessions, arts and creative venues) with the goals of both socialization for survival and political activism in contexts that reconstitute community othermothers—even if only temporarily. Our kitchen table is a movable one, but it is one in which we remain the constant throughout the critical four year matriculation period. We stand in the gap of millennial daughterline injury and loss of the motherline corps. We reach hard for those who want to be healed and mothered in this way.

Finally, we also honor among this daughterline—their visions of leadership. Rather than expecting them to embody our feminisms, we learn from them what they view as the critical issues of their time. As womanist educators we have only succeeded when we validate the standpoint they bring as millennial women. Indeed, this is critical to the generation of a line of defense that is capable of facing down twenty-first century challenges and cultural productions that aim to smother critical thinking that is informed by womanist and critical theory. Ultimately, we stand in the gap of the daughterline's needs for mother nourishment. Ostensibly, we design pathways for their development, and we applaud their outstanding efforts to emerge from the wilderness of patriarchy to craft a feminism of their own!

[1]Generation X encompasses those individuals born between the period of 1965 and 1981. Generation X has 46 million members which makes up about 20 percent of the U.S. population and is comprised of the following ethnic makeup: American Indian 1 percent; Asian 4 percent; Hispanic 12 percent; Black 13 percent; White 70 percent (see Thielfolt and Scheef).
[2]Millennials—According to the Pew Research Center (2010), the terms millennials and new millennials describe those individuals currently between the ages of 18-29 and younger.
[3]New Millennials encompass Generation Z born from 1995 through the millennium and those born at the tail end of Generation Y (see Thielfoldt and Scheef 143).
[4]"Mothering the mind" is a concept originating with Elsa Bark-

ley Brown and further theorized by feminist scholar Patricia Hill Collins (*Black Feminist Thought*). The term mothering the mind refers to the relationships that can develop between other mothers and other women wherein a mentor-student or mentor protégé relationship and a sister bond is created.

[5]Rhetorical Constructed othermothering is the oral or written discourse that is intended to nurture, educate, protect, socialize and promote individual and group well being all of which promotes the welfare and survival of a race (Conway 7).

[6]Talented Tenth—W. E. B Dubois describes the critical role and function of the African American intelligentsia led by scholars, leaders and culturalists, in "The Talented Tenth," from *The Negro Problem: A Series of Articles by Representative Negroes of Today.*

[7]Proprietary college is the language we view as more preferable than "for profit" college. Proprietary college refers to the category of institutions of higher learning that are neither state funded publics, nor independently endowed privates, but rather provide an education in which the lion's share of funding comes directly from the matriculants.

[8]All names and identifying information has been changed to protect the confidentiality of any individuals referred to throughout this essay. All quoted text is paraphrased by the authors.

[9]Alaycia's narrative comments are provided here for further context: "Mother-King, you have to know my story to understand me. I was raised by my grandmother, because of the substance abuse that took my mother's life ... and kept my father [intermittently] in and out of a series of health crises. Gram had already raised her own kids and some of my siblings. Most of the time she raised us all single handedly without the support of a male partner. She is my heart. She's always given me unconditional support. But even she could not keep me off the streets and away from some of the bad influences. I had a temper and would go at it with anyone who offended me. Somehow I made it through school and got into college. I decided I didn't want a dead end life and I couldn't hurt Gram by dying before my time. So I promised myself that my life would be different if I could give back some of the love she had showered on me. I wanted to help girls like me whose lives could easily go astray with abuse, incarceration, or death. I wanted to

start a school, or create a social program. Then I got here [college] and I kept hearing people say I don't write, talk or think well, and don't even know what I know. It was so painful that I almost fell back on my old ways of drinking, drugging, and fighting. But since I'm committed to changing I refused to backslide. So to really go forward I need to be mothered through a relationship with you. Even though it's selfish I need you. Can I work for you? I'll do it without pay. Let me just sit at your feet so that I can learn what it truly means to be a woman and a scholar. Gram and Auntie are good women, but they know nothing about college life. I've presented at a conference, studied abroad, and attended a summer research program.... I'm doing things they will never do. I'm hungry for that mothering that says that I'm okay as a black woman and that I'm going to make it."

[10]Quotes from our data that demonstrate the moments of insight students have include: "Oh. Yes! I get that because Mrs. So-and-so in my neighborhood was just like that!" or "Mother So-and-so at my church was one of those community leaders." Or even, "I have an example of what it was like to be one of 'Ella's Daughters' because my teacher selected me to work on a voter registration service project where we attended meetings and a series of pre-service trainings together. She really schooled me on the process."

[11]Excerpt from Teraya's interview narrative: "I work hard to be seen by my black peers as legit. Some feel that, I'm that girl that does the feminist thing but is still down with the cause. One black student told me that the only reason that I received a very prestigious award on campus was because I was 'in' with the white professors who liked me and my feminist work on campus! That really hurt me. But I also experience tensions from white students and other feminist students on campus. They invite me to participate in so many things to engage a woman of color perspective. But it's exhausting to be that solo voice of women of color on campus. So I feel torn in answering the call for womanist/feminist and racial diversity. How do you choose where to place your energies? I'll never be a person who seeks a completely safe way out because I like the tensions that my subject position creates. I push the boundaries of any group I'm a part of. I'll always try to get each sector to stretch and be less homogeneous. I like to mix it

up by bringing my white friends to the BSU functions; and getting my black friends to come to mainstream events. But it also makes me feel vulnerable and depleted. If we could just talk sometimes it would help me sort out people's reactions to me. I'd love to just talk through some of the disappointment and isolation that comes with the label of black feminist on this campus."

[12]Scholars have identified the phenomenon of "acting white" as a label that adolescent and young adult blacks place on their peers to pressure them to disregard standards of behavior that will gain favor among whites. Interestingly, scholars of racial identity development find that once issues of racial identity are resolved in progression to adulthood, the perception and labeling of others as "acting white" all but disappears (Spencer and Harpalani 7).

[13]The following narrative from Maya expresses her views: "I'm a feminist, I just don't go around saying it. My mother was abused and so was I by my stepfather. During my sophomore year, I was in an emotionally abusive relationship. It was so devastating that I considered suicide. Since then I've fought for my own recovery to get on stable ground. By having gone through such pain, I know that my work in the world is to empower women and girls in building their self-esteem. You know that I started a black women's 'on campus retreat' where we share, affirm each other and do our hair, and nails. As a spoken word artist, I create campus performances on feminist issues celebrating black women's strengths. Thanks again for designing our leadership sessions. But I am sad that as I prepare to graduate, still so many women on campus don't get it. They don't identify as feminists or grasp the implications of running each other down, withholding support, fighting over the few men on campus, and gossiping. Pushing the spirit of sister bonding is hard work. But it is so important that I plan to keep it going in my career as a social worker."

WORKS CITED

Barkley Brown, E. "Mothers of Mind." *Double Stitch: Black Women Write about Mothers and Daughters*. Eds. P. Bell-Scott, B. Guy Sheftall, J. Jones Royster, J. Sims-Wood, M. DeCosta-Willis and L. P. Fultz. New York: Harper Perennial, 1991. 74-93.

Belenky, M. F., L. A. Bond and J. S. Weinstock. *A Tradition that Has No Name: Nurturing the Development of People, Families and Communities*. University of Virginia: Basic Books, 1997. 11-12.

Collins, P. H. "The Social Construction of Black Feminist Thought." *Signs: Journal of Women in Culture and Society* 14.4 (1989): 745-73.

Collins, P. H. *Black Feminist Thought: Knowledge, Consciousness, and the Politics of Empowerment*. New York: Routledge, 2000.

Conway, C. B. "Rhetorically Constructed Africana Mothering in the Antebellum: The Racial Uplift Tradition of Mary Ann Shadd Cary." *The Journal of Pan African Studies* 2.1 (1989): 7-8

DuBois, W. E. B. "The Talented Tenth." *The Negro Problem: A Series of Articles by Representative Negroes of Today*. Ed. Booker T. Washington. New York: James Potts & Company, 1903. 31-76.

Evans, S. "Women of Color in Higher Education." *Thought and Action* 23 (Fall 2007): 131-138.

Ferguson, S. A. and T. C. King. "Going Down for the Third Time." *Mothering in the Third Wave*. Ed. Amber Kinser. Toronto: Demeter, 2008. 166-86.

Higginbotham, A. L. *Shades of Freedom*. New York: Oxford Press, 1996. 3-7.

hooks, b. *Teaching to Transgress: Education as the Practice of Freedom*. New York: Routledge, 1994.

hooks, b. *Bone Black: Memories of Girlhood*. New York: Henry Holt, 1996. 160-162.

Kubow, P., D. Grossman and A. Ninomiya. "Multidimensional Citizenship: Educational Policy for the 21st Century." *Citizenship for the 21st Century: An International Perspective on Education*. Eds. J. J. Cogan and R. Derricott. New York: Psychology Press. 2000. 133-135.

Ladner, J. *Tomorrow's Tomorrow*. New York: Doubleday, 1972. 110-112.

Ogletree, C. *All Deliberate Speed*. New York: W.W. Norton & Company, 2004. 6-13.

Smith, B. "Introduction," *Home Girls: A Black Feminist Anthology*. New Brunswick, NJ: Rutgers University Press. 2000. xxxii-xlvii.

Thielfoldt, D. and D. Scheef. "Generation X and the Millennials:

What You Need To Know About Mentoring The New Generations." 2005. Americanbar.org. Web. Accessed: October 28, 2014.
Williams, Patricia J. *Seeing a Color-Blind Future: The Paradox of Race. The 1997* BBC *Reith Lectures*. New York: The Noonday Press of Farrar, Straus and Giroux, 1997.

Other Mothers in Motion

Conceptualizing African American Stepmothers

DEIDRE HILL BUTLER

THIS ARTICLE DESCRIBES how African American stepmothers employ Patricia Hill Collins' other mothering framework in their daily lives. Previous examinations of stepmothers have been couched in the sinister unemotional model, made plain in fairytales with no consideration of racial diversity, while African American family scholarship has normalized stepmothers as an element of fictive kinship relations. Both notions neutralize the diversity of role conflicts, cultural expectations, and agency African American stepmothers assert. Hence, engaging another mothering framework, as articulated by Collins, allows for a more comprehensive understanding of contemporary African American stepmothers lived experiences. The other mother framework articulates a shared, communal, or assumed mothering responsibility that is empowering and inclusive of social transformation for stepmothers and their chosen children. Multiple informants gave in-depth interviews or responded to an online survey where their challenges and strategies were explained, and other mothering practices became evident. This closer analysis of daily lives of African American stepmothers, adds to the growing literature about the complexity of step mothering in American family structures, and demonstrates how a growing number of African American stepmothers navigate their roles.

The study also explores how African American stepmothers reconceived of their approach to black motherhood. African American stepmothers engage Patricia Hill Collins "other mothering" ethic in their daily lives. Although many experts claim that the black divorce rate outpaces that of whites, the General Social Survey (GSS) finds that the two groups are actually quite similar. According to Tom White of the GSS, which is funded by the National Opinion Research Center at the University of Chicago, about 36 percent of Blacks and 34 percent of whites have divorced. Despite the fact that divorce and remarriage rates for African American males have risen, very little is known regarding how the women these males remarry construct their parenting role. The findings are such that, African American stepmothers enact nurturing maternal practices, countering deviancy stereotypes of stepmothers, while accepting responsibility for a child that is not biologically her own.

A variety of deviancy discourses derive from this ideological construct of mothering—the main description of motherhood is of a married heterosexual woman in a biological nuclear family. Those who do not conform to the script of full-time (biological) motherhood in the context of marriage are viewed as deviant; single mothers, welfare mothers, minority mothers, immigrant mothers, lesbian mothers and stepmothers—often overlapping but not mutually exclusive categories—are subjects of deviancy discourses of mothering (see Fineman; Kurz; Sidel). Therefore, African American stepmothers challenge the deviancy discourse, because they slightly cross the boundary of what is deemed as normalcy in cultural circles, due to the assumption of biological motherhood in community institutions. Yet their process of motherhood is outside the normalized trope. African American stepmothers put in motion other mothering through their consistent nurturing stance, while simultaneously, countering the notion that stepmothers are wicked. By highlighting the other mothering strategy, African American stepmothers can be viewed in a way that is considered normalized in black motherhood studies, while challenging the singular nuclear biological model of motherhood. Thus, challenging the marginalized status of multiple forms of motherhood.

Collins explains that other mothering "consists of a series of constantly renegotiated relationships that African American women experience with one another, with black children, with the larger African American community, and with self" (Collins *Black Feminist Thought* 176) Feminist standpoint theory urges researchers who study women to place women's lives at the center of analysis in order to gain a better understanding of them, and how sociopolitical structures impact their lives (Collins *Black Feminist Thought;* Harding). Standpoint theory examines the lived experiences and sociopolitical stage of African American stepmothers as they reconceived their parenting strategy as a combination of other mothering and challenging the negative depictions of stepmothers. The negative stereotype of stepmothers as less nurturing, interlopers in literature and personal consciousness present an influence for the conception of African American step mothering performance and practice. Therefore the confluence of everyday reflections of African American stepmothers coupled with the sociopolitical influences of this phenomenon begin then to engender the mothering discourse of African American motherhood studies, and step mothering practices generally. While earlier work using standpoint theory emphasized women's common experiences, current work, including the present analysis, recognizes African American stepmothers conflicted relationships with the institution of motherhood; where cultural strings of other mothering is expressed and often met with opposition inside family framework, all the while being ignored in community settings. Our intersecting identities coupled with motherhood status, creates the potential for different standpoints among women (Harding). A fundamental tenet of standpoint epistemology is that the standpoints of women and others marginalized by intersecting systems of oppression (i.e., race, class, gender, age, sexual orientation and mothering status), emerge from positions from which they are able to see, not only their own positions, but the dominant system as a whole. This view from the margins is often referred to as the "outsider within" perspective (Collins *Black Feminist Thought, Fighting Words*).

The "outsider within" perspective for African American stepmothers is in part due to the cultural value of fictive kin and normalizing extended family into African American family. The fictive kin and extended family models are celebrated and resourceful for overcoming economic and political barriers historically, yet they pose a conundrum for African American stepmothers who are confronted with role ambiguity. This role ambiguity is then fueled by the assumption of instant love and nuclear family bonding from various community sources and oftentimes self. Therefore, exploring

African American stepmothers as other mothers provides another intricate layer of understanding a growing number of black women's lives, and how they enact other mother beliefs, while interacting with perceived assumptions of the stepmother role.

In the present analysis, I use a Black feminist standpoint framework to explore African American stepmother social locations. Collins argues that a Black feminist standpoint emerges from African American women's location as outsiders-within systems of domination, and directs attention to African American women as self-defined, self-reliant individuals confronting race, gender, and class oppression from society including black family frameworks (my emphasis). From the vantage point of the outsider within, African American women have created an independent, viable, yet subjugated knowledge concerning our own subordination and strategies for empowerment. Collins leans on Nancy Hartsock's description of standpoint theory, which argues that knowledge and ideology are shaped by social position, Collins points out that the interdependence between consciousness and experience has given rise to a unique self-defined black feminist standpoint. This African American stepmother feminist standpoint articulation is embedded in the double public box for African American stepmothers. She is either evil or invisible. Invisible in black family discourse because she has been absorbed in an assumed seamless role of fictive kin family caregiver. Yet the instant love myth is prevalent. While the caregiver, nurturer role may ring true to the process of enacting that role, that roll is still mired in political and social action, and spiritual grit which is both self-imposed and socially constructed. This article unpacks the realities and lived experiences of African American stepmothers through recounting oral interview data. The present study places African American stepmothers at the center of analysis, to reveal knowledge about African American stepmothers from their standpoints.

CONTEXTS FOR AFRICAN AMERICAN STEPMOTHERS

According to recent data 18 percent of African American children live in a stepfamily. A growing number of these stepfamilies are made up of a biological father and stepmother. Sociologists defined a stepfamily as a household in which at least one of the spouses had a biological child from a previous marriage. However, the term is being defined more broadly now—a stepfamily is a household in which two adults who are biological or adoptive parents with a child from a previous relationship elect to marry or cohabitate. The United States Census defines a stepfamily as a married-couple family household with at least one child under age 18 who is a stepchild (i.e., a son or daughter through marriage, but not by birth) of the householder. Researchers claim that stepfamilies face a number of issues when they attempt to merge two households after a remarriage or established cohabitation (Benokraitis). The three main issues are; developing the stepchild-stepparent relationship, establishing closeness and cohesiveness, and helping children adjust to this new family structure. These issues confronted by African American stepmothers incorporate both the instant love myth and instant family myth. Both myths assume positions for the stepmother, in that, she is supposed to inherently nurture and aid her new family through the next phase of this relationship, and at the same time, remaining aware of her own values.

In practice, African American stepmothers who enact an othermother ethic bridge personal and political activism, not only for the sake of self, but also for the sake of culture and family. African American stepmothers who adopt an othermother ethic align with Katrina Bell McDonald's contention that *mothering is activist in nature, due to its collective and empathic nature* (McDonald). The foundation of other mothering is nurturing children through collective means and community-determined ideals. African American step mothering is part of the community mothering discourse, which provides a protective sphere of encouragement and cultural understanding for youth and for the women themselves. In addition to this, mothering practices are often the basis for community-based political activism (Gilkes). According to bell hooks, black women's struggle against racism (and sexism) infuses their mothering practices inside and outside of their "homeplace; hooks refers to the homeplace as a "site of resistance." (She explains, "working to create a homeplace that affirmed our beings, our blackness, and our love for one another was necessary resistance." Hence, other mothering embodies how

African American stepmothers perceive their sense of home, and their modes of parenting as sites of resistance to the blurriness of a stepmother role through implementing other mothering values. The idea of step mothering is well grounded in the other mothering ethic, although lived expression of this idea still has its tensions. Building a stepchild-stepparent relationship, establishing closeness and cohesiveness, takes time to adjust. Yet, African American stepmothers find power in the ethic of other mothering even in the midst of the struggle for creating these new relationship bonds. This article elaborates how African American stepmothers conceive their stepmother role and enlist another mothering ethic into their daily lives as a strategy to balance the ambiguous role of stepmother.

BACKGROUND

In the spring of 2001, I became a stepmother and as a scholar of African American women's activism in personal and private spaces I wanted to know more about other African American women who had decided to take on this role. During the fall of 2004, I began interviewing African American stepmothers about their perceptions of family and their roles as stepmothers. The initial group of nine women between the ages of 28 and 83 were from the Boston, Massachusetts and Albany, New York areas. They come from diverse economic backgrounds; one woman is transitioning from welfare and returning to low-wage employment. The others, with exception of a retired 83-year-old domestic worker, are employed in professional jobs ranging from New York State employment to hospital clerical work to real estate brokerage. All of them were born in the northeastern part of the United States with the exception of the 83-year-old, who is from Tennessee.

After gathering information from my first-tier informants, with the assistance of the information technology staff at Union College, I designed a web survey and launched it in May of 2005. To date, I have received 82 responses from women of African descent from all over the United States, ranging in age from 28 to 55. Of these 82 women, 32 percent have earned a Bachelor's degree, 29 percent have earned a Master's degree, and 15 percent have earned PhDs. Forty-four of them live with their stepchildren full-time.

Sixty-eight percent of them earn $75,000+ a year and 21 percent earn $50,000-$75,000, while seven percent gross below $50,000. When asked if they participated in paying for child support or other financial obligations, 65 percent said yes, 33 percent said no, and 2 percent did not answer. This quantitative data, however, does not convey the emotional management step mothering entails and the incorporation of other mothering in their daily lives. Therefore this article is an analysis of a select portion of responses to questions related to intersection of African American step mothering and other mothering.

CONCEIVING THE STEPMOTHER ROLE

Thirty-six-year-old stepmother of a thirteen-year-old child describes herself as African American, Caribbean and Native American and describes her definition of a stepmother:

> *First, we do not* EVER USE, AND HAVE NOT EVER USED THE TERM STEP-. *A child of the village is a child of the village so my son has been my son since the day I met him—even though he has a birth mom too.* [her emphasis]

This stepmother conceives of her role as an othermother from the start. She infuses the other mothering ethic in a way, which forms a interlocking bond between her and child she has chosen to mother. A 32-year-old African American stepmother to a fifteen-year-old girl and eight-year-old boy from Minneapolis, Minnesota states:

> *Culturally I do believe in the classic phrase "it takes a village to raise a child." I feel my role in the village now to these children is to commit myself to their wellbeing. My experience has been all adults involved love all the children involved and there is no difference made between them. Culturally I think this ideology is distinctly African American and as a consequence African American, the extended family is the family, now I am a part of their extension.*

A 31-year-old African American and Caribbean descent woman

stepmother of one eight year old boy discusses her understanding of why there is acceptance or normalizing of African American stepmothers and blended families overall in black culture, "I do believe that in general the African American community has a higher tolerance and acceptance of non-traditional family structures."

These stepmothers present the othermothering ethic through her cultural lens of connecting the love she has for her chosen children to the political and social collective function of the family. Her commitment to her children is drawn from the value of keeping family members nurtured and connected. A position of self-sacrifice is evident in this stance as well, yet she finds fulfillment in knowing her efforts are part of a collective process of cultivating family. A Detroit Michigan stepmother provides health and dental insurance through her employment and other incidentals like cloths and recreation. She is 46 and has one stepson. She conceives stepmothers to be, "someone who loves their child and takes care of that child as if that child were their own, unconditionally." Fifty-one-year-old African American stepmother from Buffalo, New York who has earned a masters degree and is a stepmother to an eleven-year-old stepdaughter and ten year old stepson agrees with the previous statement:

> *When I was growing up every woman on the street as well as my parents' female friends and female relatives were a sort of "mother" in that I knew they had my best interest at heart when interacting with me. Initially, I brought (that) attitude into my role as stepmother—like the idea of being universal mother/aunt.*

The attitude is a key ingredient in the other mother stepmother. This Buffalo native believes and enacts her belief of collective mothering as essential to her stepmother role. It is of value to her and she places high status on expressing that belief in her notion of mothering. Forty-two year old African American Stepmother from San Antonio, Texas comments on her conception of a stepmother. Her image of a stepmother is a person who is responsible maternal figure who set rules and held children accountable for their actions. Thirty-nine year old African American Stepmother from Virginia who holds a PhD and is a stepmother to two males 14 & 16 and one four year old female enacts her other mother stepmother approach in her own experience with her extended family. "Because I grew up in an extended family environment, I really dismiss the notion that I am a stepmother." Thirty-six-year-old stepmother of a thirteen-year-old boy describes herself as African American, Caribbean and Native American and describes how her cultural values influence her step-mothering outlook.

> Interviewer: How has your family upbringing influenced your step mothering?
> Informant: *Significantly. I'm very old school African American I believe that every child deserves a chance and that means that every child deserves to be mothered and if it does not come from the birth mother then it should come from some 'other mother in the village' this was how I survived. This ethic of communal care was passed on to me by my other mothers...who were all academicians, preachers, and teachers they also cooked cornbread, prayed, and taught me how to change diapers.*

Other mothers connections throughout community spaces; in the school, healthcare institutions and religious places supports an interconnected other mother ethic (McDonald). African American women who adhere to the value of collective community mothering and other mothering agree with the action of care and nurturance outside of biological ties. Hence, other mothering is shown through an engaging discourse of aid.

CULTURAL CODE OF AFRICAN AMERICAN STEPMOTHERS

These excerpts frame another mothering code for African American stepmothers. These statements connect the loose borders African American stepmothers negotiate while attempting to other mother in the midst of an ambiguous stepmother role. The societal image of a stepmother and the cultural ethic of other mother places African American stepmothers into the traditional stepfamily dilemma of assuming instant love from all parties involved. Understanding that stepfamilies rarely have a model to follow and that many norms and values are colliding at once time and communication is necessary for harmony to develop. Stepmothers receive pressures from their partners and put pressure on themselves to seamlessly become motherly towards their children and not question their role. The other mother ethic helps in the process because it undergirds the lessons that family love takes time and negotiation is not instant. Other mothering is work and takes effort. Thirty-five year old New Jersey stepmother of two girls ages two and eleven and one boy age five states that her husband assumed the *instant love motif*; which means he thought she would instantly love the children as furiously as he does. The assumption is a classic stance within stepfamilies (Benokraitis). The love grew while she enacted a loving and nurturing approach. Even though the kids thought she was just trying to win them over at first. Consequently, it took years of adjustment for a family rhythm to occur which enable her to display her other mothering values and for the children and her husband to believe her approaches of care. Step-family specialists counsel stepfamilies to enable them to understand that a bonding experience is not solely a destination but a journey that takes effort from all members. Hence, the cultural code for this African American stepmother was embedded in patience and not being deterred by the slow bounding process. A thirty-nine year old African American stepmother from Philadelphia, who cares for two stepchildren one girl (thirteen) and one boy (eight) states, "Stepmothers are there to assist with the rearing of a stepchild. Not to replace the birthmother in any way, or to take away from the relationship that the child has with the birthmother." The code here is marked by a cooperative spirit between stepmother and birthmother and the ability to be open to building a relationship of trust and for the wellbeing of the children involved. Therefore structuring a "homeplace" for all members of the family unit and building a solid footing as a stepmother. Thus, challenging the ambiguity of the role and enlisting a consistency within the reframed family unit. Thirty-one-year-old African American stepmother of an eleven-year-old girl from New Jersey elaborates on how the other mother ethic is vibrant within her family notion. "In my family, everyone was considered a potential family member, my cousins' close friends would attend our family reunions, and my girlfriend is family. We are pretty big on inclusion. I see that in all Black families, usually. There is no distinction between step, non-family, etc."

Thirty-eight-year-old African American stepmother with one 20-year-old stepdaughter from Baltimore, Maryland surrounds her step mothering experience with the "other mother" code. "My cultural background has made it easy to accept my role as a step mother so I never struggled with the concept. In my household, people often lived together that were not related by blood yet considered themselves a family." Thirty-one year old African American stepmother of an eleven year old girl from New Jersey elaborates discusses her standpoint about step mothering while expressing an othermother spiritual lens. "I used to get depressed that my oldest didn't actually 'come from me.' But none of my children are mine anyway. We are just stewards for God. All children belong to the Creator and must return to Him." The common theme throughout these testimonials is the codes of patience, cultural awareness and spiritually grounding in their approaches to how they incorporate other mothering into their stepmother role. The inclusion of all people into the family fold is essential here. Also, the viewpoint of helping to care for and nurture children, while supporting the cohesion of the family unit is strongly expressed in these reflections. The focus on the children is essential. The stepmother puts herself in the role of co-nurturer and steps from the spotlight to enable the care of the child or children to come first while keeping the family consistent. This idea is expressed poignantly by a Fifty three year old African American stepmother from Trenton, New Jersey, with two male stepsons, 37 and 35, and one birth son, 32, reflects on her how she exercised her other mother code throughout her step mothering. "We put the children at the center and made them the focal point. The concept of women coming together to rear children is very typical in our culture. I believe for many of us it is stamped in our DNA."

Forty-nine-year-old African American stepmother from California, birth mother to a 22-year-old daughter and stepmother to three males and two teenage females expressed how her cultural background and family structure growing up influenced her awareness and practice of other mothering that became her road map for how she approached her stepmother role. "Because I was raised in a predominantly female environment, you always take in children and take to children. I just thought would have been helpful as well as my mother was a stepmother, so I just assumed some things." The credence to hooks' *homeplace* theme is evident in the excerpts. hooks explains, "...working to create a homeplace that affirmed our beings, our blackness, and our love for one another was necessary resistance." These statements reflect on how African American stepmothers perceive developing and maintaining homes framed in consistent nurturance and support for all members.

Thirty-five-year-old Detroit, Michigan native describes her step mothering in action.

> *I think the Black family has strong family values. And I really felt strongly that I wanted to be a good stepmother to my stepchildren, especially the one who lived with us. I was responsible for him on a daily basis and new that I would have more influence on him than his own mother. I took that role very seriously and wanted to give him everything he needed to be happy and content. I think our culture naturally lends itself to having extended families. My parents and sisters reached out to my stepson as part of the family.*

Forty-year-old Atlanta, Georgia, stepmother puts her step mothering code into practice by purchasing the birthday and Christmas gifts. She also contributes to purchasing school clothes for her nineteen- and seventeen-year-old stepchildren. Her stepchildren are also on her health insurance and dental plans.

Thirty-five-year-old New Jersey stepmother of two girls ages two and eleven and one boy age five sums up her stepmother practice through recounting the consistent activities done together. "I try to have Friday as our day. We watch movies, bowl, etc. It's just me and them." Fifty-two year old Bronx, New York stepmother navigated the pressures of the assumptions of instant love by taking on the role of being a friend. The approach most stepmother counselors and scholars advise (Benokraitis): "Being a stepmother seems more like being an older friend."

These excerpts display how African American stepmothers renegotiate their relationships by nurturing in varying degrees. Hence putting the multifaceted layers of mothering into play based on the other mother code and reinforcing as Collins explains that other mothering "consists of a series of constantly renegotiated relationships that African American women experience with one another, with black children, with the larger African American community, and with self" (Collins *Black Feminist Thought* 176) Another pressing theme for the African American stepmothers in the study was the presence of the media and how it negatively portrays stepmothers. The Cinderella stereotype factors into their conception and practice of other mothering into their stepmother role; they actively used other mother to refute the Cinderella stereotype. The stereotype asserts an evil interloper stepmother portrayal (Dainton).

CINDERELLA'S LEGACY: INSIDE THE STEPMOTHER ROLE

Stepmothers are inundated with to negative media driven depictions in popular culture. Fairytales and major motion picture films depict stepmothers as threatening and sinister; most notably the stepmother portrayal in Cinderella. The stepmothers are portrayed as evil/wicked women who are motivated by greed and resent the children in the home. As evidenced below African American stepmothers have internalized the stereotype. African American stepmothers choose to challenge it with their other mother ethic. Challenging the deviancy notion of the stepmother stereotype with another mother ethic adds stepmothers to the black motherhood discourse. The excerpts display the acknowledgement of the stereotype and real life strategies to combat it. Thirty-five-year-old African American stepmother of a nine year old girl and birth mother to a four year old and seven year old girls from Detroit, Michigan explained her image of a stepmother in negative terms: *interloper, stingy and mean*, and a 34-year-old stepmother of from Ashland, Virginia, agrees she thought the image of stepmother was *an interloper.* While a 51-year-old stepmother from Atlantic City, NJ, assumes she was *influenced by the "evil" stepmom portrayals in society.* Forty year old Atlanta, Georgia, stepmother of two thought poorly of stepmothers before becoming one, I thought stepmothers were "mean, controlling and abusive" based on what I saw in the media. The quotes above are examples of how the negative and ungenerous stepmother image is part of the mindset of African American stepmothers yet they still choose to challenge it with other mother actions. Thirty-five-year-old New Jersey stepmother of two girls ages two and eleven and one boy age five states thought that stepmothers were "*mean, evil, not valuing the children and selfish.*" She challenged her own negative stepmother image when she became one and took the approach of showing care through the phase of acceptance from her young stepchildren which took years. A 32-year-old African American stepmother who grew up on military bases all over the United States and Europe had a double lens experience with step mothering. She had the living image of her own mother as a stepmother and she reflects on that and more. "The image I had was the traditional "step monster" image. I grew up seeing how my mother treated her stepchildren and I don't think she was very nice to them. Therefore, I grew up not wanting to be a stepmother. Once I became one, I told myself that I would treat my stepdaughter the same way I treat my own children and also treat her the way I would want my daughter to be treated in the same situation."

ROLE AMBIGUITY

A 39-year-old from Memphis, Tennessee, describes a challenge confronted while raising her 14- and 20-year-old stepchildren, "different parenting skills between each parent. Spouse child rearing ideas totally different from yours. Coming into a child's life and trying to change or undo things taught or not taught. Some examples are manners, respect and integrity. Family members (grandparents) involvement contradicts your rules. They are too involved which confuses the child. Yet the triumphs of being a stepmother are having another child to love and nurture. Learning to love unconditionally. Learning to do things differently than before with child rearing. Learning that all children are different and can't be handled the same. It doesn't matter if a child is blood related or not, you still love them like your own. The same love, blood, sweats and tears you put into your biological ones is the same that you put into the ones that are *not*." Thirty-eight-year-old African American stepmother with one 20-year-old stepdaughter from Baltimore, Maryland, describes a role strain within a social institution where one often finds support. "In this case it wasn't the institutional pressure that caused angst it was just the newness of the stepmother role that brought in trepidation yet with time and effort the role strain subsided. At the beginning, however, I did feel embarrassed at church and other social gatherings to talk about my stepdaughter, especially since except financially we weren't playing an active role in her life."

Fifty-three-year-old African American stepmother from Trenton, NJ, with two male stepsons, 37 and 35, and one birth son, 32, reflects on the early days and times of struggle and role ambiguity,

> *The birth mother is the first mother. I believe it is the stepmother's responsibility to figure out how to support and guide the children without overshadowing the birth mother. Initially, my stepson's mother was very negative. But over time, when she saw we both had the boys' best interest at heart, she mellowed. Over the years we established a solid, cordial relationship and have been able to deal very effectively at weddings, baby births, and other family gatherings. She is Nana, I am Grammy and we're not confused.*

Thirty-five-year-old African American stepmother of a twelve-year-old male and eight-year-old female and birthmother of twelve-year-old twins from Detroit, Michigan reflect on the struggles and negotiations it takes to balance the stepmother role and family configuration. "The balance of attention between my biological children and my step children has been a challenge; learning how to be a companion and not a "mother" to them. Other challenges include different rules in different households, discipline or lack thereof. Allowing the paternal parent to interact with the children and not taking on added responsibility. Chores and self care for themselves when they are in our home. Biological children feeling like special treatment is being placed on step-children while they are here. Some triumphs include reaching a happy medium with communication with their parents, children getting along without fighting."

Thirty-three-year-old African American stepmother of a five-and-a-half-year-old stepson and birth mother to one son from Harrisburg, Pennsylvania, describes an emotionally charged role strain moment which still exemplifies an other mother framework,

> *Since both children are in my household the majority of the time, I find it difficult to love my stepson the same way I love my birth son. I try very hard to make things appear equal, but in my heart they are not. I struggle to provide my stepson the same level of care and concern I give my birth son. I struggle not to be annoyed with his personality quirks that remind me of his mother. I struggle to incorporate him in my Mother-Child interactions. For example, many of my friends have children around the same age as my biological son, so when we get together for play dates; I sometimes find it difficult to include my step son. My friends sometimes exclude him as well. They think of me as having only one child, not two. By the same token, my stepson now calls me "Mommy" and I think of him as my son. I am growing closer to him every day and a stronger bond is forming. I include him in my shopping and in my thoughts and plans of family activities. I take a lot of the initiative as far as his schooling, extracurricular activities, etc. In other words, I do many of the same things for him that I do with my birth son [18 months old].*

Fifty-one-year-old African American stepmother from North Carolina who is a stepmother to one 35-year-old young lady, reflects on her early days as a stepmother and the swift transitions that often take place as part of the ambiguity of the role,

> *What I had not planned was that once we were married,*

the biological mom would send her to live with us. That was a tremendous adjustment...newly married and now having a thirteen-year-old daughter who was dealing with the trauma of "desertion" from her mother. There was a real twelve-month or so adjustment period ... husband feeling guilty ... adolescent girl with so many feelings! But with prayer, being positive, honest it worked out. We are best of friends. She later added during the rough times.... Finally the stress of me trying to make it work and she at 13 being a little rebellious caused me some medical problems ... ulcers. After that diagnosis, both of them tried harder to make our family work. And it did.

These excerpts demonstrate complexities of the other mother ethic and patience to exercise it is clear. A true component of the other mother ethic is an understanding that it takes commitment and strength with a vision toward maintaining family relationships. As bell hooks asserts, "working to create a "homeplace" that affirmed our beings, our blackness, and our love for one another was necessary resistance." Hence, other mothering embodies how African American stepmothers perceive their sense of home, and their modes of parenting implements other mothering values.

CONCLUSION

An other mothering framework, as articulated by Patricia Hill Collins, allows for a more comprehensive understanding of contemporary African American stepmothers lived experiences. Embracing the ethic demonstrates the agency of African American stepmothers as community mothering activists and should place African American stepmothers in the black motherhood discourse. The black motherhood discourse has rich examples of African American activist mothers who wield a communal stone at nurturing youth in various social locations (McDonald). The other mother framework articulates a shared, communal, or assumed mothering responsibility that is empowering and inclusive of social transformation for stepmothers and their chosen children. This closer breakdown of contemplation and practice by African

American stepmothers adds to the growing literature about the complexity of step mothering in American family structure and demonstrates how a growing number of African American stepmothers conceive and practice their role. This work also pushes the experiences of African American stepmothers from the margins to the center of black motherhood studies and includes their struggles and ingenuity of crafting a daily practice from a rich cultural template. Understanding the complex lives of African American stepmother renders another visible layer of black women's lives evident and meaningful.

WORKS CITED

Benokraitis, Nijole V. *Marriages and Families: Changes, Choices, and Constraints*. Upper Saddle River, NJ: Pearson Education, 2007.

Butler, Deidre Hill. Unpublished African American Stepmother Oral History Archive. 2012.

Collins, Patricia Hill. *Black Feminist Thought: Knowledge, Consciousness, and the Politics of Empowerment*. 2nd ed. **New York: Routledge,** 2000.

Collins, Patricia Hill. *Fighting Words: Black Women and the Search for Justice*. Minneapolis: University of Minnesota Press, 1998.

Edwards, Arlene. "'Community Mothering': The Relationship between Mothering and the Community Work of Black Women." *Journal of the Association for Research on Mothering* 2 (2000): 87–100.

Dainton, Marianne. "The Myths and Misconceptions of the Stepmother Identity: Descriptions and Prescriptions for Identity Management." *Family Relations* 42.1 (1993): 93.

Fineman, Martha Albertson. *The Neutered Mother, the Sexual Family and Other TwentiethCentury Tragedies*. New York: Routledge, 1995.

Gilkes, Cheryl T. *If It Wasn't for the Women: Black Women's Experience and Womanist Culture in Church and Community.* Maryknoll, NY: Orbis Books, 2001.

Harding, Sandra G. *Whose Science? Whose Knowledge? Thinking from Women's Lives*. Ithaca, NY: Cornell University Press, 1991.

Hartsock, Nancy C. M. "Standpoint Theories for the Next Century." *Women & Politics* 18.3_(1998): 93-101.
hooks, bell. *Yearning: Race, Gender, and Cultural Politics*. Boston, MA: South End Press, 1990.
McDonald, Katrina Bell. "Black Activist Mothering: A Historical Intersection of Race Gender and Class." *Gender &Society* 11.6 (1997): 773-95.
Sidel, Ruth. *Keeping Women and Children Last*. New York: Penguin Books, 1996.

Black Motherhood and the Power of the Intersectionality Framework

A Midwifery Perspective on the "New Racism"

KARLINE WILSON-MITCHELL AND VINCIA HERBERT

MODERN CANADIAN SOCIETY is considered by many to be the utopian nation of tolerance, inclusion and diversity. In addition, an essential tenet of the Ontario midwifery model is "woman-centered care" (Maputle). However, there is limited research describing the experiences and desires of Black women upon which care is to be centered. Limited research exists describing the lived realities of women of color and their relationships with the Canadian healthcare system. There are several studies documenting inequitable access to health services and privileges in general (Patychuk 39-40; Enang 154-7). In this sense, women of the African Diaspora share similarities with other women of color who are oppressed due to sexism, class, racism and immigration status. Patricia Hill Collins provided the language with which to define the intersectionality of oppression, the rubric to measure it, and the critical social theory to study it. This chapter is authored by a midwife educator and midwifery student in the spirit of intellectual partnership and co-creation of knowledge. Although we lament the prevalence of White privilege that exists in the educational and healthcare systems, as a student and educator, the authors of this chapter humbly acknowledge our own privileged positions as first generation Canadians whose parents endured much sacrifice to procure our access to quality, elite, and postmodern education. Thus, we benefit from a level of integration into the dominant Canadian culture that many of our new immigrant sisters have historically been excluded from.

This chapter will first describe the context of intersectionality from which a Black midwife healer and academic observes motherhood. The general healthcare system and multicultural community that provide the backdrop for the narrative of Black Canadian mothers will also be described. This is relevant, because in a postmodern Canada that claims to be a "color-blind" society, institutional racism remains. This chapter will present the preliminary peek at the outcomes of a qualitative study of Black Canadian mothers, first and second-generation immigrants to Toronto from the Caribbean. An analysis of the phenomenon of Black motherhood will follow, which will utilize intersectionality, Black feminism and social justice lenses. Finally, the voices of Black mothers will be retold using the language of the bereaved. This chapter comes full circle in retelling a story of loss, hope, struggle and resilience, not unlike the story of the Greek mythological figure, Demeter. Women of the African Diaspora who find themselves on Canadian soil cry out no less for their lost children, their lost opportunities and their lost innocence.

IDEOLOGICAL FRAMEWORK OF A BLACK MIDWIFE HEALER

As researchers and academics, we find that it would be more comfortable to begin this chapter by quoting epidemiology and American population statistics. The reader might then be swayed by the impact of a minority group that suffers 2.5 times the preterm birth rate and maternal death rate than its dominant majority counterparts (Hauck et al. 209). One might be alarmed by the apparent health disparities, lack of access to social and health resources, or lack of social justice afforded to achieve the social determinants of health as the World Health Organization and the Centers for Disease Control have recommended. Unfortunately, birth outcomes of Black Canadians are neither measured nor studied in Canada, though current researchers report that these statistics are vital to equity research (Bierman, Shack and Johns 5, 10, 26, 45). Nonetheless, these would merely constitute a collection of numbers. Rather, we would argue that the story of Black motherhood is best told by the Black women themselves, recorded not by an outsider, but by Black women from the same communities, who themselves are familiar with discrimination, oppression, and cultural incompetence.

Just as scholars have argued the credibility and value of Patricia Hill Collins published works, delivered in the language of the oppressed instead of the language of academics, they may have also questioned the value of her accounts of personal narratives that introduce the reader to her work such as, *Black Feminist Thought*. Similarly, we pondered about the relevance of admission that our research does not pretend to be "objective", since no researcher embarks on research without a worldview, theoretical framework or socio-political perspective in mind (Tesh 4-6). As a Black midwife and novice healer, our goals have much to do with the promotion of equity. Consequently, our model of disease causation would avoid blaming Black women or their communities for their higher rates of maternal death from heart disease (often seen as a condition that is modifiable by lifestyle) (Creatore et al. 781-9). We search for other reasons to explain the birth outcomes that we observe. Perhaps these outcomes have developed from the woman's life, history, socio-political and biological heritage as the "life-course" proponents posit (Hutchison 375-6). In fact, Amnesty International argues that the disparate rate of maternal death following cardiovascular incidents amongst Black, Hispanic and migrants should sound an alarm (1-4). The preliminary research about the possible effect of psychosocial stress on women pre-conceptually, during pregnancy and labor (Wadhwa 17-29) warrants further investigation.

Another phenomenon that puzzles so many maternity care providers is the fact that so many well educated, socio-economically stable, well-nourished Black women continue to have higher rates of preterm birth (less than 37 weeks) and low birth weight babies (less than 2500 gm) than their White counterparts. According to Jesse et al., almost "…18 percent of African American infants are born preterm compared with 11.3 percent of Caucasian infants and 11.8 percent of Hispanic infants. The reasons for these racial disparities are largely unknown, and adverse birth outcomes among African American women remain after controlling for economic factors" (Jesse et al. 35). The emerging research surrounding health disparity and the federal efforts to provide benchmarks by which to curb institutional inequity in health care, in Canada and the U.S., are not enough (National Quality Forum 2-3; Patychuk 26-34). Black mothers themselves need to make their stories heard. Powerful truths may be uncovered through research steeped in critical narrative inquiry (Webster and Mertova 3-6). For this reason, the stories of six formally educated and resourced, Black Canadian mothers follows. Intersectionality is used to analyze the discontent noted within the narratives, and to connect their suffering with those of less resourced Black Canadian and American mothers.

BACKGROUND: CANADIAN MULTICULTURALISM

Beginning with enslavement, Blacks from either the continent of Africa or from the United States have resided in Canada for over two centuries. The newest Black immigrants originate from North and West African nations, the Caribbean, Central and South America.

With the passing of the 1988 Canadian Multiculturalism Act, Toronto has become one of the world's most multicultural cities, with immigrants making up over 45 percent of the population at the last census (Chui et al). More than 50 percent of Canada's visible minority population lives in the census metropolitan area of Toronto (2.2 million), with Blacks comprising the third largest visible minority group (Chui et al; Citizenship and Immigration Canada). The Black population of 352,200 made up 16.2 percent of Toronto's visible minority population, and 6.9 percent of its total population. Approximately 195,300 (55 percebt of the Black population) were foreign-born from the Caribbean ("Facts and Figures"). Notwithstanding Toronto's pluralism, Black communities continue to report disparities, racism and discrimination with respect to labor issues, education and healthcare services (Bierman, Angus, Ahmad, Vahabi, Glazier et al. 127-129; Williams et al. 14-18). However there are few studies that document these experiences amongst Black mothers.

It is therefore relevant and timely to explore the experiences of women of color who access maternity care services and resources in Toronto. The authors acknowledge the social nature of the terms "race," and the subjective nature of the terms "ancestry," "heritage," and "ethnicity." Despite the focus on Caribbean and African immigrants in this chapter, the authors recognize that globally, South Asian and Indigenous peoples similarly report experiences of discrimination related to skin color.

RESEARCH METHODOLOGY

This research study examined the pregnancy, labor, and post-natal experiences of Black women in Toronto with the intention of expanding knowledge with practical applications within the scope of Ontario midwifery and Black feminist theory. Phenomenological, feminist, post-colonialist, and community-based frameworks were used for data collection and analysis. Through participant interviews and personal reflections, information on several topics was gathered, including: choice of and relationships with primary caregivers; laboring experiences; place of birth; initiation (and duration) of breastfeeding; and factors that facilitated or hindered access to maternity care. By collecting these narratives, we hoped that further analysis would capture some of the diverse and intersecting identities found within Toronto's Black communities.

Following are findings and analysis that may be compared and contrasted against the experiences of other Black mothers of the African Diaspora and the larger population of Canadian mothers. Some of the participants described barriers and challenges in maternity care; however, others experienced empowering births within the healthcare system. Prior to data collection, the authors admitted to a Black feminist worldview, and attempted as much as possible, to simply listen to the interviews with caution not to add personal views or experiences to those of the respondents. It is noteworthy, however, that following the interviews, respondents reported a sense of relief, solidarity, support and caring simply because the interviewers provided a safe space to reveal their most private sufferings and joys of motherhood. We found that the post-Collins and neo-liberalist world continues to struggle with disparity and social injustice amongst Black mothers that are not easily addressed in the mainstream Canadian feminist movement.

PRELIMINARY RESULTS OF THE BLACK MOTHERHOOD STUDY

Six women of the African Diaspora were interviewed in a pilot study. The following themes emerged following initial analysis of transcripts. Each mother was college-educated, middle-class, having birthed one or more children within the previous five years in the Toronto area. This study provides a valuable contrast to the American studies of primarily poor, marginalized, Black American women. The women described a total of eleven births that were attended by obstetricians, midwives and nurses. They also described postnatal and newborn care that was managed by midwives, obstetricians, family physicians and pediatricians.

A continuing theme was the concept of birth that was worthy of suffering. The suffering was described in the forms that were common to most mothers, including labor pain, sleep deprivation, body image and lifestyle changes. Following are samples of responses describing the mother's feelings, thoughts and experiences.[1]

> *Well ... it was a life-changing experience.... One of the things that I've been struggling with for a long time is exhaustion ... on a daily basis. I felt overwhelmed a lot of the times. And you know, it gets a bit frustrating, because I look around me, yes, there's so much to do but not enough time. And I worked right up until two weeks before I gave birth, so I find myself falling on my desk and snoring ... because I've been so tired.* (P3)[2]

What made these themes unique to the Black women in the narratives was a common thread of emotional and psychological suffering stemming from unfair or disparate access to information and opportunities.

Occasionally suffering was described as enduring discriminatory treatment, unequal access to natural or innovative labor management techniques, isolation during painful and frightening experiences, withholding health promotion education, unexplained and harsh enforcement of rules upon partners.

> *Not me, but I think my partner did experience that*

> *[racial discrimination] while we were at the hospital. I think one nurse, she was very rude to him. Because he's been on the road back and forth and he's working ... he's trying to, you know, visiting me at the hospital and then working at the same time. And being on the road driving. So he was a bit exhausted when he came.... And later on he needed to use the washroom and he went into the washroom and she was like, "the washroom is for patients only!" Her tone of voice. She could have said it in a better manner, her tone of voice. So he felt, he felt really bad. And you know, here he is, and you know, his partner just had a baby and he's here to support me. And the nurse is treating him that way. And he felt like complaining to management or the person in authority about it. And I told him, I'm not here for much longer, just pray about it.... Yeah, he said she was very rude and he [found] it quite disrespectful.* (P2)

There was an assumption that, had they been one of the "other women" (White women), the caregivers may not have assumed their compliance with paternalistic or medicalized birth.

> *Honestly, I think for the first time, I felt discriminated against. I know that they were busy. I actually was saying ... if a few people called in sick I'd be sympathetic to that. But she said no. They were staffed properly. So that means they ... didn't care that I was put to the bottom of the list.... There was no one of my race at all. It was Asian, White and Pilipino.* (P1)

Two mothers made allusions to infringements upon autonomy and agency. One sub-theme was that of "withholding what others usually get." Two mothers noted that their experiences of midwifery care provided them with greater agency than their experiences with obstetrician-lead care. These findings are particularly pertinent when considering that each of the women held provincial health insurance that equally entitled all mothers and recognized residents to universal maternity care services during pregnancy and birth.

Yeah. Because it starts at the beginning. You decide to have a child so you are decision making and your—I guess I could use the word— autonomy starts from the beginning. So once you have that, that extends into the delivery and the birthing process. When you are in a situation where all of the decisions are being made for you, you don't know what's going on. When you get to the hospital, it's the same thing. You don't know what's going on. The decision is being made for you. And you sometimes walk out of there feeling robbed. So, you know, I felt a little robbed [laughs]. (P5)

The women placed inherent value upon the personhood of the infant and the bond or attachment to their baby that involved protection, responsibility and joy.

As I told my mom, I thank you for raising me and putting up with my foolishness. It's the hardest job in the world, I don't care what anybody says. I've been in some really disgusting, bad, hateful environments. And I'd say raising up my son is the hardest job in the world.... I've worked in ... stressful environments ... in the media, I used to work in a lot of things. And raising up my son is the hardest. And I guess it's because I'm struggling to be the mom and I guess the wife as well. But at the same time it's the hardest job, it's the most rewarding job. Because at the end of the day, I look at him, he smiles, he laughs, he looks at me and he says "mom," he says "mama" or "dada." ...Those days are the best. (P2)

I would just take a look at [son's name] ... it's like planting a seed ... starts to germinate and split open. And then the transformation begin[s].... So it's like you looking at something wonderful before your eyes ... blossom into something beautiful, and you feel proud. You feel accomplished. ... He's jumping up and down and he's healthy his skin is beautiful. He's strong. His weight is perfect. And I felt that I'm ... doing an excellent job as a mother. So it's a sense of accomplishment.... Yeah, I'm so proud.And my mom tells me that]and a couple of my friends as well. (P3)

Other motherhood constructs emerged in the women's descriptions of their relationships with their own mothers and included intimacy, passing on knowledge, wisdom and friendship. Women described the importance of care providers in their integration into the motherhood role. Although the mothers each had high expectations for themselves as autonomous, capable and responsible mothers; they conceded that this was the most vulnerable time of their lives and subject to tears and grief for the loss of the lives that preceded the birth. This theme was consistent with previous research (Bourgeault, Benoit and Davis-Floyd 8-9). The study findings likewise echoed the general birth literature illustrates how women also shared feelings of anger, grief and loss over their anticipated care and the care that was received.

I was trying to ... go through this process as long as I could without any medication. 'Cause as I say, I did martial arts and I have a high tolerance for pain, so I said let me try to tough this out as much as I can. And I tried as hard as I could. So ... I found out the hospital had a Jacuzzi ... I'm like, "that's exactly what I want. Let's do this!" ...I stayed in the Jacuzzi tub for about two-and-a-half hours.... he nurse gave me a shot in my thigh.... And like after awhile, I just, I had enough of it ... so I came out.... I should tell you when I first came out the nurse was like pushing epidural. Like that was the first thing she was—the first thing. And I just kept saying "No. No. No. No, I don't want it!" I wanted this on my own—if I could just do it myself without any pain medication. She was like every time, "You ready yet? You ready yet?" But my hairdresser told me that the reason they push for the epidural is it's easy. Easy shift... you don't keep tending to her [the patient]. I was like, "Are you serious?" That's crazy! (P2)

They valued the support of partners, care providers and friends. They received what was considered helpful guidance and education from community support groups, the Internet, family members or allied healthcare providers that were not directly involved in their maternity care. They placed great value on the care provider's role as educator and informant.

> *Yes, my mom ... and my husband [provided me support]. Then what happened was, I did at certain stages experience a little baby blues. 'Cause when I had all of the hormones and stuff and then the weight gain, I tore so to use the washroom was very painful. And two of my friends came by, 'cause ... I'm on Facebook as well. So two of my friends came by because I wrote, "I haven't eaten"; or "I've barely had food, barely ate today." So my friend's like, "What! What's going on?? ...It was nice, those two girls checked up on me every now and then.* (P2)

> *[A community group was] a good resource ... other practitioners would come in and share resources and you could just talk and we had more time. 'Cause you know when you go to, even your midwife, your own doctor, you only have like 15 or 20 minutes, or whatever the case may be. With them, you're able to sit down and talk. We had tea and you know, other additional questions were answered. That was helpful.... I would recommend [it to] other people.... Yeah, if they had information sessions, which are, instead of giving information to one patient at a time, one couple at a time, to make it a group session.... So everyone's there asking various questions and making it a social thing. And [it's] also because a lot of women are not working during that time so it gives them somewhere to go.* (P1)

By contrast, women also expressed concerns about time management challenges that were overwhelming at times both during and after pregnancy. One woman reports her antenatal care as mostly positive and the typical visit lasted ten to fifteen minutes providing time to return to work.

> *It was a good experience.... I get in and I get the test*

> *done, or speak with my OB. And I head back to work. So it became a routine.... Yes it was very welcoming ... it made me feel good to go to my doctor ... even though I knew what she was gonna ask me already ... because it became so routine.... Yes. She's a very neat and organized and kind of, what should I say ... she's very efficient.... I was well pleased.* (P3)

There was also a theme of spirituality within the birth experience that seemed linked to reverence, coming of age or rite of passage. The atmosphere of reverence during their labor experience could be marred by their perceptions of disparate healthcare or uncaring providers. Many times women made reference to a deity protecting them through the experience, despite the perceived deficiencies of their healthcare. The women saw their motherhood role as one that was a noble or sacred trust. It involved the impartation of knowledge, choice, protection and opportunity to their child. None of the women described the need for a ceremony, cultural ritual or spiritual practice during their birth. There was however a described need for timely words, respect for silence and empathy from a caregiver that "connected" with them in a deep way. None of the women described the involvement of a spiritual leader, however mother-figures such as aunties, grandparents, in-laws and friends acted in the role of confidante. One woman described the involvement of a close friend's mother as one who provided secret, healing knowledge for pregnancy discomforts and natural herbal induction, reminiscent of the traditional healers found in Indigenous cultures.

> *And her [roommate's) mom was living with us. After a certain period of time she was staying with us for a couple of months ... but she was like the mom of everybody, you know. She was always there, she would just listen to provide um support in terms of advice, you know, motivation, she was very helpful in terms of the natural aspect of it. Because she's very healthy, she's a reflexologist. So she's very tapped into the spirit, body and ... she was just great. I loved her!*

> Interviewer: And that sort of being "tapped into the spirit and the body" was very important to you?
>
> *Oh yeah, yeah. Even with my son, I mean, he was born ... he was four days overdue. And I was like, I need an oil, I need a remedy or something, 'cause this is not working out. [Chuckles]. And she was like, "Okay. Get...." She gave me a whole list of oils. She said to get some sage ... some lavender oil.... But she was like, "You mix this; you put this on the bottom of your feet, in this particular area, this one on your back." It was just really great. "And get yourself some raspberry leaf tea." And I did all of what she said and the next day I was in labor. So it was good.... Yeah! It was very effective!* (P5)

This same mother described a need to "own her labor" by using her scented candles, her music, her own home and her own perceived "safe place."

> *[Loud sigh] How did it change my life, I mean, having a child changes your life, right? Like I think with my daughter, I felt empowered—I have strength.... I don't know if it was the birth itself or actually having my daughter or both but I felt really strong, after I had her. Qnd with my son ... even though I did not have the delivery that I wanted, I had the labor that I wanted. I did not want to be in a hospital all hooked up to stuff. I just wanted to be at peace, at home, in my own shower, my essential oils and my candles ... rocking, moaning ... yoga.... I just did my own thing, and I felt really good. So it, it just changed my life in a sense that I feel that if there's something I want to do, no matter what it is ... I know that I'll have the willpower and the determination to do that. And every time I'm out with my kids, it gives me strength, you know. My little babies [whispers almost reverently].* (P5)

From three of the participants, there emerged a sense of being the recipient of stigma or stereotyping by the actions and words of maternity caregivers or the public. The emotional responses ranged from resigned angst to anger.

> *The thing is that because I'm a Black woman and I look really young [participant is 34 years old], I noticed with a lot of people, for example, when I was pregnant [and] went to a maternity store to buy things, and like I said, I'm a Black woman and I look young, so a lot of people assume I'm just another single Black woman, kind of like, you know, I'm not married or anything. A lot of times I would like see someone looking at my ring finger to see if there's a ring there or not. And sometimes, when I was pregnant, I didn't wear my ring a lot because my fingers got swollen.... I couldn't [wear a ring], they [fingers] were too fat. And sometimes I had a little discomfort, like I got a rash or whatever. So I didn't wear my ring sometimes. And you know one day I was making a purchase at the maternity store and I saw the woman look at my ring finger. And she purposely looked. So, I'm like, "give me a break, I've got a husband." I tried to say that I'm married and stuff ... but that happens a lot.* (P2)

These statements could stem from ageism or the mother's own insecurities. However, it appeared to the mothers that the association of youth, lower socioeconomic level, ill intent and powerlessness was often made. It made them feel vulnerable. This begs the question of whether statements of youthful appearance might not be racially coded words, similar to other statements, for example, "I have a Black friend" or "You speak so well [for a Black person]."

> *I can't say that I have [noticed any discrimination]. I mean, with my daughter my doctor was Black so [laughs] ... it was like talking to a family member ... only thing was when I gave birth to my daughter, I don't think it was related necessarily to my color, but they just thought that I was young [participant is 30 years old] or you know what I mean ... like I was bullied.... "We know. We're the health professionals." But I was like, "I have a degree. And so I*

> *know a little bit about the body. I know what I'm feeling." You know what I mean? "And that I'm not signing for a cesarean section so, I'd have to pass out before you're doing that!"* (P5)

These statements reveal a level of societal perceptions, stigma and stereotyping at large. Months and years following these experiences, these issues evoked tones and expressions of disappointment, indignation and anger. In one case the indignation provided the impetus for a mother to establish a service business with the aim of providing helpful aides and clothing that would assist women in labor. The items were Afrocentric in nature. She stated that "... these are the things I wish someone had told me that I would need." Health disparity and perceived injustice can become catalysts for protest and civil action.

CONCEPTUAL ANALYSIS EMERGING FROM BLACK FEMINISM AND SOCIAL JUSTICE FRAMEWORKS

Patricia Hill Collins argues that the time for civil disobedience and protest may have given way to a new type of militancy, which expresses itself in the narrative of hip-hop. Indeed social media, music and film have been harnessed at various times to galvanize support, mobilize mass social action and to express the angst of Black people. However, within the larger narrative landscape, there is a hitherto little heard subplot. Popular media does not seem interested in Sojourner Truth's proclamations: "Ain't I a woman? ...I have born 13 children and seen most all sold off to slavery ... and when I cried out with my mother's grief, none but Jesus heard me.... Ain't I a woman?" (Clift 58). Is Sojourner's cry of loss in motherhood too painful a message or too powerful a challenge to the complacent?

In *Black Sexual Politics*, Collins describes the media portrayals and White perceptions of Black women as animalistic, uncivilized and sexually wild (27). She also describes how performance art is defiantly marketed to sell these images; even to extent of the language and lyrics employed by the Black artists and song writers. Collins alludes to perceptions of Black motherhood by White

America in her chapter on motherhood, "Will the 'Real' Mother Please Stand Up? Race, Class, and American National Family Planning" in her book, *Black Power to Hip Hop: Racism, Nationalism and Feminism* (55-74). Here she describes the dominant White view of Black mothers as undeserving of the prized and sacred title of "mother," and therefore not entitled to the social and societal privileges of motherhood (55-58, 65-67). She traces public policies that would appear to limit anti-discriminatory labor laws and health policies that render fertility treatments and family planning services inaccessible for Black American women. The perception of the undeserving, less than sacred Black mother could very well be the worldview behind health disparity observed in both the American and Canadian healthcare systems.

Supposedly, women's rights and health reproductive movements (Morgen) achieved momentum in both White middle-class and non-White (and non-middle class), feminist circles. If that were the case, one would have expected that freedom of self-determination, dignity and respect would have been afforded to all women during pregnancy and birth. Women may have access to "family-centered," luxury-type maternity wards and labor suites in our hospitals. Innovations such as exclusive breastfeeding (Kramer 63-4), partners cutting the umbilical cord (Mercer 58) and "skin-to-skin" care of infants (Gray 1) have become easier for hospitals to accommodate. But sadly, despite the diversification of the manual of the battle cry, *Our Bodies, Ourselves*, Black women and Black feminists ways of knowing, and ways of birthing, have neither been fully respected, nor incorporated into the mainstream of maternity care. In a sense, the "new racism" (Wane "Black Feminist Theory" 7-9) in the birth place is polite and palpable although segregation is invisible.

Some Black midwives in the U.S. have begun to document and to study the work of Black healers, the use of Centering Pregnancy® group prenatal care (Rising) as a culturally safe method of care delivery and the need for provision of a safe space in which Black women may realize the choices provided (J. Joseph). However, there are few Black researchers, archivists, midwives or healers to record the culture, health beliefs, historical and current desires of Black mothers or to inform health policy that could address gaps in care. Some Black mothers speak to the need for symbols and community to support and welcome newborn infants, not unlike Aboriginal or Indigenous peoples. However, just as the memories of Aboriginal birth have been lost to many communities, Afrocentric epistomology of birth and newborn welcoming have been lost. If not the ancient pre-colonial birth practices, then newly identified, postmodern African diasporic healing and birth knowledge could provide cultural safety for today's Black mothers and families. It is often assumed that by living in a multicultural society that purports to tolerate everyone, and working in a healing profession which values caring, no one people group or subculture is left wanting. To assume this fallacy is to disregard the intersectionality of race, culture, class and socioeconomic status in the oppression of mothers. Some would go as far as to say that health disparity will always exist, and must always be addressed. And in some continuum, all sectors of society are connected in our intersecting identities. So as long as there exists anyone who is oppressed, we are all oppressed. Even within the Black communities of Toronto, there are further intersections of oppression based upon religious heritage, sexual orientation, history (or life course), immigration and settlement experience, length of residence and level of integration within the greater Canadian society. In fact, many authors describe the term "immigrant" as really a "code" for racialized groups and explain that Canadian opinion polls probably measure hidden racist attitudes in the guise of describing Canadian values and lifestyle according to Patychuk (30).

Njoki Wane, a Black Canadian feminist researcher, describes Black feminist theory as a "convergence of journey in a central place whereby people are differently located in terms of class, sexuality, language, and ethnicity ... [and that] the contemporary experiences of Black women ... [are] both an oral and written epistemology that theorizes our experiences as mothers, activists, academics, and community leaders. It can be applied to situate Black women's past and present experiences that are grounded in their multiple oppressions" (Wane "Black Feminist Thought" 38). Informed by her qualitative study of over 1,000 Black women across Canada with origins throughout the African diaspora, Wane speaks to the Black Canadian experience. From both individual and focus group interviews, themes that emerged from this research included: 1) Narratives that are credible because they come from Black women; 2) A distinction between academic feminism and community activist feminism; 3) The relevance of immigration and settlement issues to Black Canadian feminism; 4) The inclusivity of strong Black mothers and sisters within the framework; 5) Postcolonialism, patriarchy and pride in national heritage as distinct from pride in race; 6) Spiritual pain and suffering, feminism that speaks to the soul; 7) Silence on issues of sexuality, risk and sexual orientation; 8) Respecting and working across difference within the African diaspora as a feminist concept (Wane "Black Canadian Feminist Theory" 145-154).

What are current examples of systemic and institutional racism? Toronto's Black mothers are at risk for discrimination in medicalized birth settings due to race, gender, socioeconomic status and the vulnerabilities encountered due to the immigration and settlement process. In North America, up until the early 1980s, it was common to restrain all laboring women in their beds or on delivery tables for birth. Reminiscent of the slave auction blocks, many Black women and adolescents were hoisted up in stirrups like carcasses of beef in a butcher's shop (Bourgeault, Benoit and Davis-Floyd 5-6). Supposedly, the enlightened era of modern "family-centered" birth centers in hospitals arrived to free women from the imprisonment they experienced in a medicalized birth, where healthcare providers were the wardens and rule enforcers. Nonetheless, many contemporary Black mothers describe a sense of being separated from services and fulfillment of dreams, in a way that denotes virtual imprisonment within the walls of the healthcare system. Although unconfined behind iron and cement walls, Josephine Enang explains that some Black mothers in Nova Scotia describe a sense of oppression akin to virtual imprisonment (154-7). These examples do not negate the health policies that support the entitlement of all women to adequate maternity care in Canada, regardless of status. Many of the cases of oppression and health disparity that are experienced by women in Canada may not be intentional. Nonetheless, through neglect, withholding of services, ineptitude or purposeful discrimination, women are the subjects of oppression in Canadian institutions.

It is notable that many Black Canadian women are well educated. In fact, the subjects of the authors' research study were largely college or university-educated women with significant cultural capital. Despite this level of education, barriers persist to employment commensurate with educational level so there remain large numbers of educated poor, working poor and a shrinking middle class amongst Black Canadians (Patychuk 28-32). Many of the mothers interviewed had gained valuable information about birth and newborn care from various media (including books and the internet) as well as family members, healthcare providers and co-workers. When asked what they believed was important for prenatal care, most answered that education about birth and orientation to the expectations or options for their birth experiences were key. Evidently, their desire for an informed birth experience was similar to the desires of women reported in the literature at large (Bourgeault, Benoit and Davis-Floyd, 8-9).

To have been educated enough to acquire similar expectations for optimal birth as women in the dominant culture would have, and yet to be denied the desired experience in healthcare institutions constitutes a systemic discrimination which hides behind the great ideals for equity and universality that the Canada Health Act promises (D. Joseph 583). Again, Black women are not the only women denied their birth place or birth experience of choice. Certainly there are many powerful narratives shared by Aboriginal mothers in Canada who are in many cases forcibly removed from their rural and remote homes, families and traditions with the intention of providing supposedly "safer" urban hospital births (Bourgeault, Benoit and Davis-Floyd 5-6). In addition, other immigrants (e.g., Filipino, Chinese, South Asian, Latin American) have provided evidence of barriers to healthcare (Patychuk 32). It is significant, however, that Black mothers often experience discrimination and inequitable access based upon gender, class, race and level of integration following immigration.

What do all these issues add up to? There is a desperate need for research that follows the narratives of the Black mother. Some of the questions that require reflection include: How do class, immigration status, level of connectivity to family, race and gender affect Black mothers' agency and autonomy? What constitutes cultural safety for Black mothers during maternity care? Black feminism in Canada has only recently emerged as a distinct movement. The synergy created by further research and knowledge translation will assist us to weave the complex tapestry that reflects the intersectionality that Collins theorized about. Hearing these stories will provide an almost voyeuristic peek into one of the most powerful, yet intimate and cherished rooms in our hearts, our birth experiences.

CONCLUSIONS

U.S. statistics show unfavorable perinatal outcomes for Black women compared to White women across indicators such as low birth weight, preterm birth rate, etc. Little is known about Canadian perinatal outcomes for Black women. Insufficient data exists regarding prenatal, labor, or postnatal experiences. The Project for an Ontario Women's Health Evidence-Based Report Study, suggests that ongoing research for Black women and women of other ethnicities is vital in achieving equity in the health care sector (Bierman et al. 33-34, 45). Although Toronto boasts such pluralistic communities, it is necessary to explore the experiences of Black women who access health services in Toronto. The works of Black feminists, Patricia Hill Collins and Njoki Wane, challenge community activists, researchers and practitioners to consider the concept of intersectionality that allows us to better study the lived experiences of a Black woman who may be subject to simultaneous oppressive elements due to discrimination based upon race, gender, socioeconomic status, religion, sexual orientation, able-bodied status, immigration status and language. Intersectionality begs the researcher to consider the interactions amongst all of these factors that may influence a Black mother's perceived sense of belonging and her access to healthcare.

Most importantly, Black feminists caution healthcare practitioners against epidemiological fallacy. This calls for researchers and practitioners to avoid the assumption that a Black woman must be feared lest she manifest the medical complications and the self-defeating social behaviors described in population-based studies and the media. Perhaps a power shift is required. Instead of treating a statistic, a Black mother could receive treatments and care that were individualized in a manner that maintains her cultural safety. Much of the philosophy and framework of the institution of modern healthcare is founded on fear. The desire for safety drives us to control the environment and to control the bodies in our care. Although it leaves the practitioner vulnerable, perhaps motherhood should be treated as a sacred institution and not an entity to be feared. So sacred is this institution that the symbols, ways of communication, and ways of caring should be sought and respected. Much of our healthcare training dictates that all care provided must be uniformly dispensed in order to be equitable. By contrast, maternity care providers informed by Black feminism seek to provide a culturally safe environment for every Black mother to voice her needs, express her identity and achieve empowerment through her individual birthing experience. Black mothers across the diaspora come from complex and diverse life experiences and realities. Consequently, equitable care does not bring uniformity but diversity. Such care requires a paradigm shift in which both mother and care provider join forces to take a journey, involving risk. With so much of the ancient African diasporic birth knowledge lost to this generation, neither mother nor provider can predict where the journey to recapture Afrocentric birth will end. However, the journey requires listening to and trusting the woman.

[1]P1 refers to Participant #1, P2 refers to Participant #2, P3 refers to Participant #3, etc.

[2]Quotations of Interview Participants illustrating the theme of suffering:

"…I actually spent, almost 48 hours in the hospital, kind of all night, unable to eat. Not the entire time, but unable to eat, and this with lying on my left side … the obstetrician said, 'We're gonna do this [cerclage].' 'Cause it was kind of difficult to stay there for all that time and not eat. Worrying about you know…." (P6)

"…Unfortunately, I still snore. I snore because of the weight gain. It's unbearable, so now my husband doesn't sleep with me. First he'll sleep with me, but then he goes. For me it's really hard." (P2)

"[I was] ravenously hungry and like bloated, tired and sore. Everything." (P2)

"I found breastfeeding and the week following my son's birth more traumatic than birth did [laughs]…. [I had] painful latching, engorgement. I got mastitis, right. I had a plugged duct. We went back to the birth centre … lactation consultant…." (P6)

"It was kind of … at home it just soaks in. Even at the hospital it soaks in, like my body has just been cut open. On many levels, I just had major abdominal surgery. I just was unprepared for that and being the type of person that I am, like you know, always on the go. It was very difficult for me to just sit then let my body heal. So I wasn't mentally prepared for that." (P5)

"So what happens now is I used to invest in myself. Now, my self-worth has gone down [Ha Ha]. And now it's all about him. For example if I have to work, first thing I do is get him ready…." (P2)

"I would say…. I think it showed me that the pathway can be very difficult but the outcome fabulous! So … that was the case with my daughter. It was a difficult pregnancy. I was off work … at home. I had a lot of quiet time, a lot of reflection. It was nerve-racking at times. Because a couple times I'd gone in, fearing I was in labor and I wasn't … but it showed me that … even though there could be difficulties and complications … in the end it came out relatively well. Cause she's perfectly healthy." (P6)

"Yeah, just seeing like your own people, you know. It made me feel comfortable, plus he's very knowledgeable and he was very friendly. He was talking to me… I don't exactly know where he was from, but uh, he was...having a great mannerism about him. And he just made me feel comfortable…. He was a Black doctor. I'm not a racist person or anything. It's nice to be with your own people sometimes. [laughs] It was just a nice experience…. I never knew that childbirth would change my life the way it did…. I had a high-risk pregnancy. I had a low placenta. And you know being pregnant, my first pregnancy, I was reading all this stuff about low placenta. I basically couldn't sleep at night. I called in sick at work, I was like, oh my God, my first pregnancy, and, oh my God, I could lose the baby, he could drop at any moment! Yeah so, like I had a lot of anxiety, so I was like, oh my God, I prayed and I prayed and prayed … definitely the prayer helped me out.

Anyways, so that was going on. So it moved on and then my pregnancy was normal. (P2)

WORKS CITED

Amnesty International . *Deadly Delivery: The Maternal Health Care Crisis in the U.S.* London: Amnesty Intenational Publications, 2010. Web. 11 Nov. 2012.

Bierman, Arlene, Avram Shack and Ashley Johns. "Achieving Health Equity in Ontario: Opportunities for Intervention and Improvement." *Project for an Ontario Women's Health Evidence-Based Report: Volume 1.* Ed. Arlene Bierman. Toronto: St. Michael's Hospital and the Institute for Clinical Evaluative Sciences, 2012. Web. 11 Nov. 2012.

Bierman, A. S., J. Angus, F. Ahmad, N. Degani, M. Vahabi, and R. Glazier, et al. "Access to Health Care Services." *Project for an Ontario Women's Health Evidence-Based Report: Volume 1.* Ed. Arlene Bierman: Toronto: St. Michael's Hospital and the Institute for Clinical Evaluative Sciences, 2010. Web. 11 Nov. 2012.

Boston Women's Health Book Collective *Our Bodies, Ourselves: A New Edition for a New Era.* New York: Simon & Schuster, 2005. Print.

Bourgeault, Ivy L., Cecilia Benoit and Robbie Davis-Floyd. *Reconceiving Midwifery.* Montréal: McGill-Queen's University Press, 2004. Print.

Chui, Tina, Hélène Maheux and Kelly Tran. *Canada's Ethnocultural Mosaic, 2006 Census.* Ottawa: Statistics Canada, 2008. Web. 21 Nov 2012.

Citizenship and Immigration Canada Research Evaluative Branch. *Facts and Figures 2010 – Immigration Overview: Permanent Residents by Source Country.* Ottawa: Minister of Public Works and Government Services, 2011.

Clift, Eleanor. "And Ain't I a Woman." *Newsweek* 03 Nov. 2003: 58. Web. 22 Nov. 2012.

Collins, Patricia Hill. *Black Feminist Thought: Knowledge, Consiousness, and the Politics of Empowerment.* 2nd ed. New York: Routledge, 2000. Print.

Collins, Patricia Hill. *Black Sexual Politics: African Americans,*

Gender, and the New Racism. New York: Routledge, 2004. Print.

Collins, Patricia Hill. *From Black Power to Hip Hop: Racism, Nationalism, and Feminism*. Philadelphia: Temple University Press, 2006. Print.

Creatore, Maria Isabella, et al. "Age- and Sex-related Prevalence of Diabetes Mellitus Among Immigrants to Ontario, Canada." *Canadian Medical Association Journal* 182.8 (2010): 781-789. Web. 22 Nov. 2012.

Davis-Floyd, Robbie E., et al., eds. *Birth Models that Work*. Berkeley: University of California Press, 2009. Print.

Das Gupta, Tania. *Racism and Paid Work*. Toronto: Garamond Press, 1996. Print.

Enang, Josephine E. "The Childbirth Experiences of African Nova Scotian Women." Master's Thesis, Dalhousie University, 1999. Web. 22 Nov. 2012.

Gray, Larry, Lisa Watt, and Elliott M. Blass. "Skin-to-Skin Contact is Analgesic in Healthy Newborns." *Pediatrics* 105.1 (2000): e14-e14. Web. 22 Nov. 2012.

Hauck, F. R., K. O. Tanabe, and R.Y. Moon. "Racial and Ethnic Disparities in Infant Mortality." *Seminars in Perinatology* 35.4 (2011): 209-220. Print.

Henderson, Jennifer J., Janet Hornbuckle, and Dorota Doherty. *Models of Maternity Care: A Review of the Evidence.* Women and Infants Research Foundation, King Edward Memorial Hospital for Women, Western Australia: Department of Health Western Australia, 2007. Web. 11 Nov. 2012.

Hutchison, Elizabeth D. *Essentials of Human Behavior: Integrating Person, Environment, and the Life Course*. Sage Publications, Incorporated, 2012.

Jesse, D. Elizabeth, et al. "Racial Disparities in Biopsychosocial Factors and Spontaneous Preterm Birth Among Rural Low-Income Women." *Journal of Midwifery & Women's Health* 54.1 (2009): 35-42.

Joseph, Jennie. Personal communication. 18 April 2012.

Joseph, K. S., R. M. Liston, L. Dodds, L. Dahlgren, and A. C. Allen. "Socioeconomic Status and Perinatal Outcomes in a Setting with Universal Access to Essential Health Care Services." *Canadian Medical Association Journal* 177.6 (2007): 583-90. Print.

Kramer, Michael S. and Ritsuko Kakuma. "The Optimal Duration of Exclusive Breastfeeding: A Systematic Review." *Advances in Experimental Medicine and Biology* 554 (2004): 63-77. Web. 22 Nov. 2012.

Maputle, Maria S. "A Woman-Centred Childbirth Model." *Health S A* 15.1 (2010). ProQuest Nursing & Allied Health Source. Web. 10 Dec. 2012.

Mercer, Judith S., Carlene C. Nelson and Rebecca L. Skovgaard. "Umbilical Cord Clamping: Beliefs and Practices of American Nurse-Midwives." *Journal of Midwifery & Women's Health* 45.1 (2000): 58-66. Print.

Morgen, Sandra. *Into Our Own Hands: The Women's Health Movement in the United States, 1969-1990*. New Brunswick, NJ: Rutgers University Press, 2002. Print.

National Quality Forum. *National Voluntary Consensus Standards for Ambulatory Care – Measuring Healthcare Disparities: Consensus Report*. Washington, DC: National Quality Forum, 2008. Web. 11 Nov. 2012.

Our Bodies, Ourselves. Boston: Boston Women's Health Book Collective, 2005.

Patychuk, Dianne. *Health Equity and Racialized Groups: A Literature Review.* Toronto: Health Equity Council, 2011. 23-30. Web. 11 Nov. 2012.

Rising, Sharon, Holly Kennedy and C. Klima. "Redesigning Prenatal Care Through Centering Pregnancy." *Journal of Midwifery and Women's Health* 49.5 (2004): 398-404.

Statistics Canada. Canada's Ethnocultural Mosaic, 2006 Census. Web. 11 Nov 2012.

Tesh, Sylvia Noble. *Hidden Arguments: Political Ideology and Disease Prevention Policy.* New Brunswick, NJ: Rutgers University Press, 1988. Print.

Wadhwa, Pathik D., et al. "Stress, Infection and Preterm Birth: a Biobehavioral Perspective." *Paediatric and Perinatal Epidemiology* 15.s2 (2001): 17-29.

Wane, Njoki Nathani. "Black Canadian Feminist Thought: Tension and Possibilities." *Canadian Woman Studies/les cahiers de la femme* 23.2 (Summer 2004): 145-154. Web. 11 Nov. 2012.

Wane, Njoki. "Black Feminist Theory: Differences and Similarities and the Question of Solidarity." *Back to the Drawing Board: African Canadian Feminisms*. Eds. N. Wane, N. Deliovsky and K. Lawson. Toronto: Sumach Press, 2002. Print.

Webster, Leonard and Patricie Mertova. *Using Narrative Inquiry as a Research Method: An Introduction to Using Critical Event Narrative Analysis in Research on Learning and Teaching*. New York: Routledge, 2007. Print.

Williams, Charmaine and Notisha Massaquoi. *Every Woman Matters: A Report on Accessing Primary Health Care for Black Women and Women of Color in Ontario*. Toronto: Women's Health in Women's Hands Community Health Centre, 2010. Web. 11 Nov. 2012.

Sympathetic Distances of Black Motherhood

Reflections on the Political Agency of Cultural Remembering

SHELLEY GRANT

THE CONCEPT OF "OTHERMOTHERING" (*Black Feminist Thought* 178) referenced in sociologist Patricia Hill Collins writings on Black sexual politics (*Black Sexual Politics*) and critiques of white feminist studies on mothering ("Black Women and Motherhood"), foregrounds a common tendency for Black mothers to informally head extended family networks. In using this term, Collins challenges normative presumptions about black motherhood expressed in works by June Jordan (1985), Michele Wallace (1979), bell hooks (1984), and other Black feminists who variously attest to the positive value in Black maternal practices. They recount various instances where Black females perform "fictive" or "non-blood" maternal roles, as in voluntary guardianship of needy children and in positions of paid service. Unsurprisingly, the narratives Black feminists differ radically from those sketched within works by mainstream white U.S. theorists and the discourses of policymakers. Notably, the Black feminist depictions challenge presumptions about the "pathological" "weakness" in Black mother-lead households, alluded to either explicitly or indirectly in seminal reports such as the 1965 *The Negro Family: The Case For National Action*, authored by sociologist and politician Daniel Patrick Moynihan.

I find Collins' responses a particularly useful tool for explaining differences in the epistemologies of family building across various races. In contesting reports of "bad" Black households lead by "mammies" or "matriarchs" (Collins *Black Feminist Though* 74-75), she calls out the "past-in-present" aspects of Black sexuality that additionally constituting a "specific constellation of social practices that demonstrate how oppressions converge" (Collins *Black Feminist Though* 11). Her reflections on Black maternal epistemologies emphasize the mutability of sexual knowledge's not only along familiar racial and economic indices but also across temporal and spatial borders. Her observations about the intergenerational accrual of sexual knowledge offer new avenues for analysing the politics of knowledge manipulation that can further demean and objectify Black mothers. In explicitly considering the temporal dimensions of racist intersectionalities, this chapter examines the perpetuation of knowledge about Black family building performances into the present day through processes of group remembering.

In analysing the political salience of knowledge circulated about family building, I review evidence supporting Collins' provocative insistence that Black maternal processes are authentically "revolutionary" (Collins *Black Feminist Though* 156). In my review of shifts in the approaches for governing multiple methods of "fictive" kinship formation, I find evidence for Collins claims about the threats posed by Black mothering to the capitalist institutionalization of protections for "exclusive parental "rights" (Collins *Black Feminist Though* 156). My review of the standing child welfare laws focuses on an analysis of standards that essentially mimic the intergenerational agency of Black mothering in creating and disseminating knowledge about kinship building across borders through various channels. In analysing inconsistencies in the understanding of kinship legitimacy for families involved in the care of Black children, I explore persistent differences in perceived value maternal performances across divisions of race.

In reflecting on the trajectories of U.S. family-building policy, I consider the works of Susannah Radstone (*The Sexual Politics of Time*) on the politics of remembering, the studies of Rick Crownshaw on the transcultural dynamics of memory and other reviews of emotions commonly associated with the cultural recognition and representation of maternal performances (Bassin). These studies on the dynamics of group memories offer unique insights into Collins underlying themes of transcultural transmission of family knowledges and the exclusion of populations from cultural recognition.

Ultimately, my review of Black maternal epistemologies furthers Collins assessments on the modern dynamics of intersectionalities carried forward into the globalization of maternal politics.

FRAMING "FICTIVE" MOTHERING AS A MULTIPLY FORMED PROCESS

In fact, Black "othermothering" is only one of several types of "fictive" mothering now routinely performed by American as well as European women. This claim follows clear evidence of significant increases in the number of families created through the key categories of externally assisted reproductive practices that include child adoption, surrogacy arrangements and medically Assisted Reproductive Technologies (commonly abbreviated as ARTs). Of these modern methods, the practice of child adoption stands out as the most comparable to othermothering for several reasons. Despite superficial differences, both involve the creation of extended family networks between non-biologically related individuals and families through emotional processes of what anthropologist Signe Howell terms "kinning." Additionally, the practice of child adoption is the most comprehensively governed of the modern methods for assisted family building, enabling a more comprehensive analysis of changes in legal responses to these processes. The comparison of these two practices I initially develop within this chapter rests upon these fundamental and, I believe, largely under-examined similarities.

As with Black othermothering, the practices of child adoption are diverse. Presently, child adoption is comprised of several forms including domestic, international, post-fostering, adoption of kin and others. Excluding the legal adoptions of kin, the overall practice child adoption is now one of the most culturally visible and well-regarded family development options available to prospective U.S. parents. It is also the most statistically prevalent method of assisted family building. A 2007 *National Survey of Adoptive Parents* (NASP) of the U.S. Department of Health and Human Services conservatively reported that an estimated 1.8 million children are adopted annually (including foreign and domestic), constituting at least two percent of all American family building practices annually. While the number of child adoptions remains smaller than natural deliveries, the practice of child adoption is now responsible for the creation of a statistically significant population of families.

The multinational growth in international forms of child adoption also influences the comparability of these "fictive" kinship practices. The NASP estimates that approximately 25 percent of all child adoptions involve the placement of foreign-born children with interested U.S. families. Unlike domestic adoptions, a critical factor in differentiating international adoptions is location of children's origin although frequently racial differences exist between receiving families and adoptees. In domestic adoptions, the criteria of race or ethnicity are most commonly used to differentiate among placements. The U.S. statistics on international child adoptions suggest a proliferation in the number of "fictive" kinships that involve the determination of appropriate standards for the care of children transculturally, if not transracially.

The fictive kinships that make up Black family building patterns are informal custodial arrangements that are not recognized under the law. The non-recognition of fictive kinships marginalizes Black family building practices within mainstream U.S. culture. Assessed quantitatively, the failure to receive legal recognition of kinships also obscures the broader prevalence informal family building models across various family building methods. In reality, there are many forms of informal family building that fail to meet criteria for legal recognition. Many of these reproductive practices involve private contracting by parents to create families where the parents and children are not biologically related. While the number of families created through various methods of assisted reproduction and fictive kinships are difficult to measure, the cultural responses to specific practices diverge significantly and are influenced by perceptions about the involved populations. For instance, the 2009 *Assisted Reproductive Technology Success Rates, National Summary and Fertility Clinic Reports* created by the U.S. Center for Disease Control (CDC), Division of Reproductive Health, reports that fertility treatments including processes involving Assisted Reproductive Technologies (or ARTs such as *in vitro* fertilization, etc.) resulted in 45,870 live births (deliveries of one or more living infants) and

60,190 singleton infant births. Similarly, a composite analysis of estimated levels of surrogacy contracting also reflects practice increases. In a 2009 analysis, the U.S. Council for Responsible Genetics interpreted data obtained from the CDC and the U.S. Society for Assisted Reproductive Technology (SART) estimated a probable fourfold increase in the number of births achieved through surrogacy arrangements between 2004 and 2008. It is difficult to accurately ascertain the proportion of these non-adoption methods that are now completed across national borders, but several reports verify that increases in the formation of non-biologically based families also extend to several cross-border practices (Shenfield et al.).

Read summarily, these statistics on multiple family-building practices support the conclusion that Black othermothering is no longer the exclusive means for creating "fictive" kinships. In reality, the growth in child adoption and other assisted practices has broadly increased the numbers of mainstream U.S. families once denounced in the Moynihan report (Chapter IV) as "weak," "pathological," and "unstable." Although not exhaustive, this brief comparison of the incidence of "fictive" family building across several methods does point to inconsistencies in presumed legitimacy of families formed through modern mainstream practices and Black othermothering. The emergence of differences between the detailed renderings of Collins and the apparent popularity and cultural acceptance of mainstream versions of "fictive" mothering begs an answer to further questions about the continued exclusion of Black "fictive" mothering performances from those legitimated under the law.

SELECTIVELY GLOBALIZING "FICTIVE" FAMILY LEGITIMACY

Figuratively, the processes of "othermothering" and child adoption similarly challenge traditionally held beliefs about kinship validity, recognition and legitimacy. Both processes unearth a persistent and well-recognized cultural dichotomy between the idealized notions of "real," "blood," and "natural" mothers and inferior types of "un-real," "non-blood," or "assisted" mothering (Gailey; Collins *Black Feminist Thought* 152-3). Traditionally, "real" motherhood necessarily means the existence of genetic, biological or blood proximities between mothers and children. Despite the fact that increases in the overall number of legitimate U.S. child adoptions may have contributed to cultural acceptance of families constituted through "non-real" connections, the legitimacy of Black othermothering remains questioned or even denounced.

The contemporary approach to adoption practice governance has broadly politicized family building practices. In the next sections, I examine the global production of racial difference through the intersection of universalized children's interests and the selective recognition of caregivers as legitimate. This study assesses the standards for family legitimacy generally before considering the impact of laws specifically regulating the transracial placement of children. A review of significant changes in the globalization of child adoption governance over the past two decades yields a fascinating view of the continual refinement in maternal knowledge. In applying Collin's approach to contemporary practices, the globalization of family building policies may paradoxically allow "past" racisms to remain "present" through a transcultural differentiation of maternal knowledges.

UNIVERSALIZING AN EXCLUSIVE RECOGNITION OF "FICTIVE FAMILIES'

Undoubtedly, the legal recognition of non-biologically based kinships contributes to increased public acceptance for adoption as a valid means of relationship building. In contrast with the relatively informal performances of Black mothering, several broader changes in the governance of adoption practices have resulted in refinements to public notions about family legitimacy that bare examination. Responding to cultural concerns about the safety of children placed in adoption practices, the current standards mandate state oversight for a broad range of child placement processes. The modern law of adoption addresses the absence of biological relatedness through an explicit recognition of the need for state intervention in family decision-making that influences the welfare of children. Furthering the English Common law doctrine of *parens patriae* in some respects, the new adoption regulations establish an explicit understanding of kinship legitimacy to ensure the protection of children's welfare interests.

The globalization of adoption process standards, through the ratification of two mutually supportive multinational accords, established a basic criterion for the recognition of family building legitimacy. Due to the informality of Black care networks; many instances of Black othermothering are not recognized as legitimate under the modern law. The first measure was the *United Nations Convention on the Rights of the Child* (1989) (or UNCRC). This widely approved measure established that the "best interests of the child" must be a "primary" consideration in decision-making involving the lives of all children. The 54 Articles of the UNCRC stipulated a broad range of provisions for the support children's material and emotional well-being as well as the protection of their interests for civil, familial and heritage claims. The focus on adoption process regulation responds to evidence of adoption process irregularities believed to unduly threaten the interests of children.

To enforce the UNCRC terms globally, the member nations of the Hague Conference on International Private Law (HCCH) ratified a second key instrument aimed at universalizing the decision making standards for adoptions completed across national borders. The *Convention of 29 May 1993 on Protection of Children and Co-operation in Respect of Intercountry Adoption*, also known as "the Hague Convention" was enacted for the explicit protection of the interests of children migrating across national borders for purposes of child adoption. The measure expanded adherence to the UNCRC standards by establishing routine reporting and monitoring protocols for the social welfare authorities charged with overseeing the child placement processes by public and private agents. Effectively, the ratification of the Hague Convention resulted in the universalization of maternal standards across cultures of families.

The erasure of borders in the laws governing child adoption may have enabled greater protections for children's interests, but it also clearly distinguished "fictive" parents as either legitimate or illegitimate. A number of outspoken child welfare advocates, social service authorities and reviewers of humanitarian law have issued praise for these measures, arguing that the standards provide an effective means to address concerns about the poor family conditions of children globally (Bartholet). Although accurate, this perspective also sets forth a more uncertain claim that knowledge about children's welfare constitutes a maternal knowledge of family building. It implies that the dissemination of knowledge about children's interests allows for the recognition of broader range of family types, possessing an equal capacity to satisfy the localized needs of children. A closer examination of these presumptions suggests that the transcultural extension of the law may, in fact, result in the continued exclusion of family populations.

This understanding of racial exclusion through globalization correlates to Collins' observations on the intimate connection between capitalist systems of production and the exclusion of Black populations (Collins *Black Feminist Thought* 242). Her point is echoed in the works of geographer Jenny Burman, who maintains that broadly termed standards of law produce geographies that can be used for racial exclusion and devaluation. Applying Burman's notion to evaluations of adoption law, the culturally "desirable" family ideal becomes interchangeable with legal designations of legitimacy (Collins *Black Feminist Thought* 179), although remaining factually distinct. More importantly, women lacking the economic means to satisfy universalized criteria for maternal care may find the family ideals nearly impossible to realize. Seen thusly, the legal standards essentially affirm an idealized representation of care that is unattainable for Black mothers already oppressed by intersecting factors of race and a lack of economic means.

Evaluating racism as a spatially defined phenomenon leads to the awareness that the universalization of laws governing maternal knowledge can alter the visibility of oppression. In reference to child adoption, the extension of family building standards shifts the scales within which maternal care is evaluated as legitimate. Such shifts in the scale of legal review are not necessarily neutral in impact. The work of critical race theorist Richard Thompson Ford insightfully speaks to the politics of sovereignty that can either include or exclude populations through a re-drawing of doctrinal boundaries. In commenting on racisms within civic representation, Ford notes that

> For any given normative justification, there are several equally justified boundaries, such that the boundary ultimately chosen is not necessarily superior to other possible boundaries. The attempt to displace political controversy with geography not only fails to resolve the political questions, but also impedes sound policy. (1367)

His statement clearly evidences that knowledge is mutable, arbitrary and laden with political and lived meaning. Ford's statement challenges the notion that reframing social problems may prove an inadequate means to redress recurring historic concerns. Ford interprets the Moynihan report to invite a call to action that is false. He suggests, along with feminist theorists Robyn Warhol-Down and Herndl Price (444), that the policies are purely symbolic in nature and may jeopardize the political agency of Blacks in undervalued ways. He questions that such a policy will practically further democratic aims to increase social equity and increase the social inclusion of Black citizens. In sum, the shifting definitions of family building legitimacy can be viewed as a distraction from efforts to practically respond to the perpetuation of chronic cultural concerns, such as the perpetuation of racial inequality in applications of the law.

MISRECOGNITION AND THE SUBSTITUTION OF "FICTIVE" ALTERNATIVES TO "REAL" BLACK MATERNAL KNOWLEDGES

The inconsistencies in public and policy interpretations of different "fictive" mothering practices also correlate to transcultural variations in understandings of modern family building. This observation relates to Ford's assertion in asserting that family building knowledge is mutable across time and cultures. It is an effort to respond to Collins claim for the need for the intersectional analyses of anti-racist projects to coalesce into "tangible political ramifications" (Collins *Black Feminist Thought* 11). Examining these points further, I recall the overarching recommendation of the Moynihan report. It is an unquestionably clear call for the use of various means to eliminate the family building alternatives of Black mothers. In the end, the report calls for social welfare authorities to help conform Black maternal practices to meet mainstream white ideals. Moynihan directly states this intent within the introductory comments of the early report

> There is, presumably, no special reason why a society in which males are dominant in family relationships is to be preferred to a matriarchal arrangement. However, it is clearly a disadvantage for a minority group to be operating on one principle, while the great majority of the population, and the one with the most advantages to begin with, is operating on another. (1367)

While he acknowledges that patterns of Black mothering may be circumstantially provoked (e.g.,"the Negro community has been forced into a matriarchal structure', Chapter IV, 3), he also clearly maligns the societal value in allowing locally directed Black maternal performances. Although initially articulated in 1965, elements of this mandate are a recurring theme in many present day discourses on the governance of fictive family building.

In particular, I am struck with the repetition of Moynihan's call for conformity rests on a fundamental fear for the loss of material and professional "advantages" for Black children in modern adoption policies. His early expression of concern for children's welfare also appears in present day policy discourses around child placement decision-making. The reported reasons for improving protections for the "best interests" of children through the globalization of well-defined family building standards mimics the aims suggested in Moynihan's report. The *Moynihan Report* effectively demanded that Black families change their family-building practices to conform to mainstream norms. Such a policy intent not only enforces the perpetuation of normative family building patterns but also legitimates the uncritical continuation of remembered processes. Acknowledging this less apparent function, the policy recommendations can be understood to culturally commemorate mainstream kinship patterns through broader policy enforcement. The continued performance of these normative memories results in legal recognition of specific relationships and kinships. At the same time, failure to comply with the policy results in non-recognition of the value in informal or fictive kinship ties. Even now, the notion of commemoration haunts deliberations on the standards used to govern non-traditional family configurations.. It points to an undervalued vitality of memorial agency in the development of transcultural family building regulations that invites further examination. In order to further an examination of the processes of remembering suggested in the themes of modern family building discourses, I consider the ruptures caused by the transnational imposition of family building ideals.

My primary interest here is to explore the criticality of intergenerational transfers of maternal knowledge that Collins (*Black Feminist Thought*) implies across her varied renderings of Black maternal epistomologies. Several recent works on the politics of group memories and the formation of memories across cultural divisions provide insights on the connections between culturally inclusive knowledge and remembered performances. They support an investigation on the intersectionalities implied in Collins remarks on "fictive" mothering practices that blends considerations of law and culture. Examining mothering as a subjective epistemology touches upon several notions raised in Collins overall challenges to the intersectional racism pervading many other aspects of Black women's lives.

Practically speaking, the children's welfare standards stipulated under the terms of the UNCRC and Hague Convention articulate norms for children's care and family building processes that are universally applied and not culturally specific. Yet, the maternal knowledges disseminated through social policy standards are inconsistently interpreted and valued across political and cultural divides in very evident and meaningful ways. Interpretive variations are a commonplace and expected component of gaining transnational compliance with multinational accords (Alston and Gilmour-Walsh). In the execution of the Hague Convention protocols, the interpretation of the UNCRC human rights standards is not uniformly understood across legal jurisdictions. According to the "subsidiary" principle, the Hague allows national variations in understandings of the protected cultural interests of children (Schmit). The laws globalize particular epistemologies of mothering across cultural divisions, yet profoundly influence the evaluation of locally developed maternal practices.

The interpretation of maternal care standards varies considerably and evidently in the governance of transracial adoptions. By definition, transracial adoptions are the placement of available ethnic minority children with suitable receiving parents of a different race. Although the term transracial is literally a geographically and racially neutral term, the majority of transracial placements involve domestic placements of ethnic minority children with receiving families best able to prove levels of economic, psychological and civil stability required for final social welfare authority homestudy approval. This difference between racially neutral construction and impact remains an irreconcilable hurdle in developing transculturally applicable standards for maternal care.

The placement of Black children with white parents has received significant scrutiny from theorists and members of the social work profession of different races (Simon and Roorda; Kennedy). Since the enactment of the *Multiethnic Placement Act of 1994* (or MEPA, P.L. 103-382.Overview.H.R. 6. Enacted October 20, 1994) and the later amendments in the *Interethnic Placement* of 1996 (or MEPA-IEP), U.S. social welfare authorities have maintained a "race-blind', or stated more generally "race neutral," preferences in family placement decisions. The stated aim of the MEPA and MEPA-IEP is to prevent considerations of parental race to impede the speedy placement of children, therefore increasing speed and likelihood of finding suitable home placements for needy children.

Most critically, the race neutral standard that prevails in the U.S. is not universally held (Alston and Gilmour-Walsh). In a striking example of the divergences in the national interpretations of children's welfare standards involving transracial placements, I note that UK authorities now interpret the UNCRC "best interests" in areas of cultural rights to mandate a "race-based" national policy for child placement (Sargent). This means that UK authorities maintain a preference for placing ethnic minority children with parents of a similar racial background. Although the specific reasons for this interpretive divergence may pertain to differences between the UK and the U.S. social welfare systems, the opposing policy positions are equally linked to the universalized UNCRC"best interests" standards. The primary difference is the execution of radically different protocols for family formation, based on interpreted knowledge about the type of care required to support the social welfare of ethnic minority children.

Before the enactment of the MEPA, the U.S. child placement policy was similar to the current "race-based" UK placement standard, which prioritized the placement of Black children with Black families. The U.S. adherence to the "race-based" standard followed a milestone statement by members of the National Association of Black Social Workers in 1972 that sharply denounced the ability of white families to adequately prepared adopted Black children for the difficulties of U.S. racial discrimination (Simon and Alstein). Following this proclamation, there was a sharp decline in the number of U.S transracial child placements throughout the 1980s and 1990s which stimulated lingering debates amongst policymakers and theorists around the appropriate standards for parenting Black children (Pohl and Harris; Fogg-Davis). The U.S. policy shift on the recognition of "race" as a fundamental difference informs a study of inconsistencies in cultural reception to "fictive" mothering by women of different races.

The notion of racial difference remains central to debates on family formation among non-biologically related individuals and influences notions of care legitimacy. The continued ambivalence surrounds debates over whether children's care can be "race neutral" or needs to respond to qualities of care that are uniquely provided by women of a particular race. The support for "race neutral" child placement preferences stem in part from clinical and ethnographic studies with transracial adoptees that suggest high levels of post-placement adjustment (Simon and Roorda). Yet, the results of clinical research on transracial child placements fail to address underlying considerations involved in the transcultural transmission of memories about mothering and care and the exclusivity implied in the communication of maternal knowledges.

THE TRANSCULTURAL BEHAVIOR OF MATERNAL MEMORIES

Departing from well-thought approaches to regulatory reform expressed in the varied works of legal pluralists, critical race theorists and critical geographers of race (Price; McKittrick and Woods),

I feel it even more important to respond to less obvious cultural processes such as remembering that may perpetuate iniquities in the cultural recognition of maternal legitimacy over time. The dynamics and behaviors of transcultural memories of families is a vast and varied topic that merits reflection beyond this reflection on Collins vision of Black maternal epistemologies. Nevertheless, a preliminary review of the qualities of memory mutability and movement permit new investigations into cultural responses to processes of memory transmission, disruption and manipulation that Collins references in various writings on Black experiences in othermothering practices.

This universalization of adoption practice legitimacy can be read as a form of transcultural memorial behavior. Memory theorist Richard Crownshaw launches a study on transcultural memory by posing a question that pertains directly to this investigation into the inequities generated by the universalization of family building practice standards. He asks, "what happens when memory, so inherently dynamic, crosses cultural borders, enters into dialogue with other memories similarly mobilised, when it is freed from the identitarian claims of group ownership" (2). The methods for materializing memories about transcultural differences may change while the materiality of memories remains intact within successive variations of remembering. Crownshaw posits that "if memory is processional, its materials must be subject to a continual symbolic investment for them to retain their memorative value, and that may entail their substitution or modification by, or convergence with, other materials and media of memory" (1-2). In this statement, he suggests that the materiality of memories such as racism can persist through attempts to reconfigure practice governance. Succinctly stated, this implies that definitions of family legitimacy are more aptly regarded as culturally relative rather than universal.

Examining another feature of transcultural memory, Crownshaw's statement points to a reconsideration of adoption governance aims. A tacit aim of the current law is to address ruptures in the transmission of conceived maternal knowledges that are traditionally passed through biological or physical proximity. In some sense, the law continues traditional norms by replacing "real" connections of biology with legitimacy. Yet, the return to traditional family norms idealized by the legal mandates is a primary concern for mainstream feminists who wish to resist a return to idealized maternal roles believed to perpetuate the subjection of women. In response, some white feminists argue for cultural acceptance of parenting models that further existing parenting patterns, but engage with idealized norms selectively in non-gendered or non-heterosexual forms (Butler). The legal recognition of a broader range of family building practices along these lines critically involves a selective engagement with or "forgetting" of knowledges. The law negotiates and mediates between differing cultural visions of maternal care through attentiveness to a range of children's needs. This is necessarily an imperfect resolution to the need to respect the transnational behavior of memories and to value the varying epistemologies of mothering.

The tensions involved in transcultural maternal remembering are most exposed, I believe, in situations of memory ruptures or the evident loss or absence of necessary maternal knowledges for children's care such as transracial adoptions. For instance, the apparent rupture of interpersonal connections between biologically-related family members and the apparent distances between family members involved in transcultural family building have incited various responses. Some U.S. adoption agencies, such as Holt International (2014), which facilitate large numbers of intercountry child placements, have launched programs aimed at helping families respond to feelings of actual physical, biological and cultural difference between parents and adopted children. Some of the most popular annualized post-adoption services are organized summer camps focused on gathering children from particular sending countries or planned family travel to sending countries, termed adoptee camps and "heritage tours" ("Post Adoption Services"). The "heritage" camps involve the participation of families formed through practices of transracial adoption in events aimed at providing cultural education and emotional support to offset the negative effects of family experiences with racism. These newly constituted performances in mainstream "fictive" family building borrow from intergenerational practices of knowledge transmission that Collins and other writers identified as "community-based" childcare alternatives commonly found in

Black communities (Collins *Black Feminist Thought* 155). The activities of the "heritage" camp tacitly mimic qualities of othermothering in many respects.

Understood in reference to trends in the governance of "fictive" mothering, Crownshaw's notions offer a deeper understanding of cultural causes for the dramatic shifts in family building governance. The memorial authority of the law parallels evaluations of the psychology involved in enforcement of various "color-blind" policies by legal scholars Kimberly Holt Barrett and William George. They attribute racially discriminatory outcomes under policies of "color-blindness" to selective legal "forgetting', as implied in the failure to prove, i.e., visible recognizable a "discriminatory intent" for action (Barrett and George). Their work speaks to the authority of legitimacy that has the capacity to render memories culturally valuable. Addressing its inverse, cultural theorist Susannah Radstone states that, "authority has become diffuse, all pervasive and unavailable as a point of identification. In this context, aggression becomes harder to acknowledge and manage" ("Social Bonds" 59). Interpreted in reference to trajectories of family building authority, her comment speaks to axes of intersectionality, previously referred to in Collins earlier works.

Despite efforts to refine and expand maternal knowledge across observable shifts in family building governance, I am most curious about the repetition of idealized knowledges about kinship care that haunt present day discourses about maternal value. In evaluating the nostalgia of maternal performances, psychologist Donna Bassin offers a conceptual consideration to break the cycle of "repetition, rather than true remembering and identification." She comments that change requires "taking forward into the present the old fantasies and feelings from the original dyad with an awareness of their origin" (Bassin 172). She addresses the continual urge to reclaim the spaces of mothering within mainstream culture through attentive processes of remembering rather than idealization. This implies the need to realize the impossibility of a return to tradition and an acceptance of loss of maternal culture within mainstream societies. In this instance, the losses mourned in nostalgic responses may multiply reference medical diagnoses of infertility, ruptures in intergenerational maternal connections, genetic discontinuities or significant spatial divides. In sum, Bassin's suggestion of nostalgia offers the possibility for authentic remembering to accompany expansions in future understandings of care. Ultimately, this suggests an opportunity to craft laws in ways that protect children's interests globally in ways that do not devalue the existence of transnational variety in maternal agency.

Drawing together these notions of memory to assess changes in the valuation of mothers and cultures of care, I note an observation by anthropologist Christine Ward Gailey about the flexibility of mothering as conceptual construct. She argues that kinship actually refers to the "construction" of multiple claims to care that imply "unspoken" rather than absolute boundaries and rules (15). The meaning she suggests easily includes both othermothering and adoption as valid maternal performances. In a related expression, anthropologist and leading U.S. adoption practice historian Judith Modell insists that mothering is constituted chiefly through a performed evidence of intent to assume responsibility. Her understanding of adoptive mothering is widely shared in contemporary U.S. culture. Modell's rendering of modern kinships highlights the development of informal and localized knowledge. The concept of maternal knowledge collectively articulated by Gailey and Modell is seamless and inclusive, rather than differentiated and hierarchical.

Extending the ideas suggested by Gailey and Modell, the kinship forms and maternal roles included in Collins' notion of Black othermothering are multiple and concurrent. The qualities of these informal family building performances challenge presumptions that the aims of family policies are necessarily neutral and universal. Instead, the inclusiveness of othermothering roles indicates the perpetuation of care within family performances that privately perpetuate alternative values, interests and needs. When private family performances differ from public policy aims, the location of "home" becomes a significant location for the perpetuation of memories that defy and resist public mandates, as suggested by Susannah Radstone. In describing her vision for transnational memory studies, Radstone distinguishes between legal and cultural forms of knowledge about home in stating that "located-ness of engagements with memories on the move" (111).

She further states that, "memories continue to be received locally although mediated across cultures of varying scales," which I take to mean that knowledges about "home" are necessarily varied. Her observations on the agency of memories in the construction of home offer an alternative means to include and recognize a broader range of maternal care memories. More significantly, this recursive view of memory flows suggests avenues to realize Collins vision of the truly "revolutionary" contributions by Black "othermothers" to the formation of globalized care practices in the present day.

WORKS CITED

Adoption USA: *A Chartbook Based on the 2007 National Survey of Adoptive Parents*. Web.

Alston, Philip and B. Gilmour-Walsh. *The Best Interests of the Child: Towards A Synthesis of Children's Rights and Cultural Values*. New York, United Nations, 1996.

Bartholet, Elizabeth. *Family Bonds: Adoption and the Politics of Parenting*. Boston: Houghton Mifflin, 1993.

Bassin, D., M. Honey and M. M. Kaplan. *Representations of Motherhood*. New Haven, Yale University Press, 1994.

Barrett, Kimberly and William George. *Race, Culture, Psychology and Law*. Thousand Oaks, CA: Sage Publications, 2005.

Burman, Jenny. "Deportable or admissible? Black Women and the Space of "Removal'." *Black Geographies and the Politics of Place*. Ed. Katherine McKittrick and Clyde A. Woods. Toronto: Between the Lines. 2007.

Butler, Judith. *Gender Trouble: Feminism and the Subversion of Identity*. New York: Routledge, 1990. Print.

Collins Patricia Hill. *Black Feminist Thought: Knowledge, Consciousness, and the Politics of Empowerment*. 2nd ed. New York: Routledge, 2000.

Collins Patricia Hill. *Black Sexual Politics: African Americans, Gender, and the New Racism*. New York: Routledge, 2004.

Collins Patricia Hill. "Black Women and Motherhood." *Motherhood and Space: Configurations of The Maternal Through*

Politics, Home, and the Body. Ed. Sarah B. Hardy and Caroline A. Weidmer. Houndmills, Basingstoke, Hampshire, England: Palgrave Macmillan, 2005.

Crownshaw, Richard. "Transcultural Memory." *Parallax* 17 (2011): 1-129. Print.

Fogg-Davis, Hawley G. *The Ethics of Transracial Adoption*. Ithaca: Cornell University Press, 2002. Print.

Gailey, Christine Ward. "Ideologies of Motherhood and Kinship in U.S. Adoption." *Ideologies and Technologies of Motherhood: Race, Class, Sexuality, Nationalism*. Ed. H. Ragoné and R. W. Twine. New York: Routledge, 2000. 11-55.

hooks, bell. *Feminist Theory from Margin to Center.* Bosto: South End Press, 1984.

Howell, Signe. "Kinning: the Creation of Life Trajectories in Transnational Adoptive Families." *The Journal of the Royal Anthropological Institute* 9.3 (2003): 465-484.

Jordan, June. *On Call: Political Essays*. Boston: South End Press, 1985.

Kennedy, R. "Orphans of Separatism: The Painful Politics of Transracial Adoption." *The American Prospect* 17 (Spring 1994): 38-45.

McKittrick, Katherine, and Clyde A. Woods. *Black Geographies and the Politics of Place*. Toronto: Between the Lines, 2007. Print.

Moynihan, Daniel Patrick. "The Negro Family: The Case for National Action." Washington: Office of Policy Planning and Research, United Stated Department of Labor, March 1965. Web. Accessed July 1, 2014.

Pohl, Constance and Kathy K. Harris. *Transracial Adoption: Children and Parents Speak*. New York: F. Watts, 1992.

"Post Adoption Services." Holt International Children's Services. Web. 21 August 2009.

Price, Patricia. "At the Crossroads: Critical Race Theory and Critical Geographies of Race." *Progress in Human Geography* 34.2 (2010): 147-174.

Radstone, Susannah. "Social Bonds and Psychical Order: Testimonies." *Cultural Values*_5.1 (2001). Web. 27 Dec. 2012.

Radstone, Susannah. *The Sexual Politics of Time: Confession, Nostalgia, Memory.* London, Routledge, 2007.

Radstone, Susannah. "What Place Is This? Transcultural Memory and the Locations of Memory Studies." *Parallax* 17.4 (2011): 109-123.

Sargent, S. "Adoption and Looked After Children: a Comparison of Legal Initiatives in the UK and the USA." *Adoption & Fostering* 27 (2003): 44-52.

Schmit, A. "The Hague Convention: The Problems with Accession and Implementation." *Indiana Journal of Global Legal Studies* 15 (2008): 375-395.

Shenfield, F., J. de Mouzon, G. Pennings, A. P. Ferraretti, A. N. Andersen, G. de Wert, and V. Goossens. "Cross Border Reproductive Care in Six European Countries." *Human Reproduction* 25.6 (2010): 1361-8.

Simon, Rita J. and Howard Altstein. *Transracial Adoption.* New York: Wiley, 1977.

Simon, Rita J. and Rhonda M. Roorda. *In Their Parents' Voices: Reflections on Raising Transracial Adoptees.* New York: Columbia University Press, 2007.

United Nations Convention on the Rights of the Child (UNCRC). Web.

U.S. Department of Health and Human Services. *Assisted Reproductive Technology Success Rates, National Summary and Fertility Clinic Reports.* Washington, DC: : U.S. Government Printing Office, 2009.

U.S. Department of Health and Human Services. *National Survey of Adoptive Parents* (NSAP). Washington, DC: U.S. Government Printing Office, 2007.

Wallace, Michele. *Black Macho and the Myth of the Superwoman.* New York: Dial Press, 1979.

Warhol-Down, Robyn and Herndl D. Price. *Feminisms Redux: An Anthology of Literary Theory and Criticism.* New Brunswick, NJ: Rutgers University Press, 2009. Print.

Nineteenth-Century Motherwork

Ideology, Experience and Agency in Autobiographical Narratives by Black Women

MARTHA PITTS

THE TROPE OF MOTHERHOOD as analyzed by scholars in major reclamation work of nineteenth-century American women writers, has been inextricably tied to whiteness, the "private," and to blood-related relationships. Carroll Smith-Rosenberg and other scholars, for example, have linked white motherhood to a private woman's culture, one marked by strong relationships among women. Another analytical framework comes from Linder Kerber, who argues that, after the American Revolution, evolving concepts of national identity was governed by the notion of "Republican Motherhood"—an ideal in which, as Kerber notes, "the model republican woman was a mother" whose service to her nation "was accomplished within the confines of her family" (58). According to Amelia Howe Kritzer, "The idea that women should exemplify, teach, and guard the spirit of the republic within the family imparted a political dimension to women's traditional roles; on the other hand, it maintained the exclusion of women from overt political participation" (150). Nonetheless, literary scholars of women's writings have consistently adopted "Republican Motherhood" and Barbara Welter's "Cult of True Womanhood" which draws on dominant, prescriptive, and gendered ideologies to interpret mostly the written works of middle-class white women from the Northeast.

The idea of nineteenth-century black mothering that operates outside of the traditional mother-child model or traverses bloodlines has been egregiously overlooked; though "giving birth is indeed a part of mothering, it is caregiving that *defines* the act of mothering, and caregiving is a choice open both to those who give birth and those who do not" (Daly and Reddy 3). Thus contemporary critical analysis that engages with the maternal is much needed, particularly with nineteenth-century maternal discourse as it relates to black women. One potentially productive point of entry is applying the concept of "othermothering," a term popularized by Patricia Hill Collins in her book, *Black Feminist Thought,* describing a non-biological women-child relationship, to nineteenth-century mothering practices. Often times, however, this concept has been filtered through the often-denigrated trope of the mediated Mammy and/or actual Mammies, who took care of white children and not her own biological offspring during times of enslavement and colonization. black othermothering then, in the form of the maternal persona as a site of agency, possibility, and authority as well as the limits of adopting such persona has been all but ignored in contemporary scholarship. Most scholars who analyze nineteenth-century motherhood have either focused on the negative implications of Mammy and her lack of subjectivity, or scholars have privileged the trope of biological motherhood in the nineteenth-century, like the infamous enslaved female narrative Harriet Jacob's *Incidents in the Life of a Slave Girl*. This book is celebrated for the nurturing and heroic power of the enslaved mother. Or, analysis of nineteenth-century motherhood has been held hostage to scholarship on Harriet Beecher Stowe's *Uncle Tom's Cabin*, where mothering is framed not only by whiteness as normative but also by sentimental ideology. It is the intention of this essay to explain and correct this oversight, and to examine nineteenth-century black mothering in fresh and focused ways. I also intend to build upon the work of Patricia Hill Collins, in the hopes of illuminating its significance to a wider critical discourse on mothering.

Collins' scholarship has introduced or has extensively been developed from a black feminist perspective and utilizes important conceptual terms such as "othermothering," "community othermothering," "motherwork," and "standpoint theory." All of these terms provide a productive way of organizing this essay, and motherwork and its three tenets of survival, power, and identity are particularly fruitful for this essay's development. With her innovative ideas, Collins undermines the binaries that have traditionally governed the discourse on motherhood (as white); for example, Collins uses the term 'motherwork' "to soften the existing dichotomies in feminist theorizing about motherhood that posit rigid distinctions between private and public, family and work, the individual and the collective, identity as individual autonomy and identity growing from the collective self-determination of one's group" ("Shifting" 47).

In the traditional way of thinking about nineteenth-century motherhood, Western society has divided the world into separate spheres—public and private, marketplace and household, and masculine and feminine where the assumption is that "male dominance in the political economy and the household is the driving force in family life" (Collins, "Shifting" 46). Though historian Linda Kerber now argues that the model of separate spheres, where women post-Revolutionary War were relegated exclusively to private space of home rather than public space of marketplace, was more ideology than an accurate reflection of the lived experiences of the (white) middle-class in nineteenth-century America, feminist American literary studies has emphasized the centrality of the concept of "spheres" as an important means of understanding the lives and fictional works of nineteenth-century white women. Collins' work on motherhood is especially important because she provides a powerful critique of white feminist theories of motherhood. Moreover, Collins' concept of motherwork as "the combination of mobility among Black and White neighborhoods as culturally distinct entities, the type of work black women performed in both settings, and the meaning attached to black women's labor in both settings converg[ing] to produce a distinctive sensibility" (Collins, "Shifting" 208-209) further problematizes the public/private divide concerning nineteenth-century concepts of motherhood.

In exploring the construction of maternal authority in three autobiographical narratives by black women who were born and raised in the nineteenth century, I am interested in "shifting the center [regarding] race, class, and feminist theorizing about motherhood" to borrow the title of Collins's essay, from mostly white patriarchal perspectives to that of black women. Patricia Hill Collins's work on motherhood provides provocative ways to think about positioning nineteenth-century women of African descent who wrote autobiographical narratives as maternal authorities. Through close readings of three texts, Nancy Prince's *Narrative of the Life of Mrs. Prince* (1850), Amanda Berry Smith's *An Autobiography, the Story of the Lord's Dealings with Mrs. Amanda Smith, the Colored Evangelist* (1893); Susie King Taylor's *Reminiscences of My Life in Camp with the 33rd U.S. Colored Troops, Late 1st South Carolina Volunteers* (1902), I analyze how nineteenth-century black women writers participated in motherwork on various levels. Arguing for a broader understanding of the maternal persona these women adopt, I do not take their silences and omissions regarding their own biological mothering as a textual and literal maternal failure. Instead, I look at symbolic, discursive, and rhetorical mothering, in addition to traditional conceptions of motherhood in these texts to demonstrate the multiple articulations of motherhood in relation to the crucial categories of class, race, and the body.

In attending to these autobiographies, utilizing both the radical and traditional elements of these works, and by using Collins' work on black motherhood, I am forwarding the conversation of challenging the uncritical acceptance of the idea of separate spheres by literary scholars, which has produced the white mother as normative and a dominant narrative displacing a more complex reality. These autobiographical narratives register the ways the narrator-subjects negotiate the concept of mothering as women's primary private responsibility and sanctioned public activity and as a vehicle for authorizing black female authorship. As nineteenth-century black women began writing their narratives for themselves, they continued to speak for their own needs as well as for those of the other members of their communities:

> We must distinguish between what has been said about subordinated groups in the dominant discourse, and what such groups might say about themselves if given the opportunity. Personal narratives, autobiographical statements, poetry, fiction, and other personalized statements have all been used by women of color to express self-defined standpoints on mothering and motherhood. Such knowledge reflects the authentic standpoint of subordinated groups. (Collins, "Shifting" 48-49)

Therefore, placing the autobiographies of Nancy Prince, Amanda Berry Smith, and Susie King Taylor in the center should yield new theories and new perspectives and move toward richer feminist conceptualizations about motherhood. In fact, using Collins' theories to analyze these works advance the call to reinvigorate black feminist literary studies, which, according to Ann Ducille "is in need of bold new ideas like those that called it into being thirty years ago" (48). Reading these texts from the perspective of black feminist maternal thought as laid out by Collins opens up areas of the text that have gone unremarked in other analysis.

Because the genre of autobiography has historically privileged some narratives (male and/or white) and excluded others (female and/or people of color), autobiographical narratives foregrounding a black woman's standpoint on mothering has been missing in feminist discourse. If one function of mothering, according to Aimee E. Berger is "understood to be instructing the child and transmitting values, then the reader is positioned to be in a sense mothered by a writer whose stories serve to bring the reader into her world view" (90). This is especially important for women like Prince, Smith, and Taylor, who are all writing from a standpoint that differs from dominant thought and who privilege their experiences and subjugated knowledge. Using Collins's theories on motherhood brings to light the voice of previously silenced subjects, revealing black feminine codes of self-representation and particular writing practices that embody and exemplify agency.

To contextualize the lives and experiences of the nineteenth-century black mothers in my study, I begin with a brief biographical sketch of the three autobiographers and then discuss the ways in which Prince, Smith, and Taylor engage in motherwork to develop a view of black motherhood that is in terms of both maternal identity and role, distinct from the motherhood practiced and prescribed in the dominant culture.

NEGOTIATING A HEAVY LOAD: MOTHERWORK AS SOURCE OF EMPOWERMENT

Beyond their common gendered struggle and the shared heritage of work and racial oppression, the individual happenings of these women's lives vary greatly, although each life has been extraordinary. Their lives read almost like intentional rejections of those aforementioned gender ideologies. Though Prince, Smith, and Taylor were at some point married, the circumstances of their lives eventually led them into experiences opposite the conventional nineteenth-century marriage plot: unreliable husbands, widowhood, and inevitable self-reliance.

Nancy Gardner Prince was born free in Newburyport, Massachusetts, a small village more than 30 miles outside of Boston, in 1799. Prince's brief narrative documents her years-long struggle to keep her siblings together, her marriage to Nero Prince, and her subsequent travel to Russia where her husband served in the Czar's court. In Russia, where she lives for nine years, Prince boarded children and sold items as an entrepreneur. Before her husband died, Prince left Russia for America because of her health, and in Boston, Prince unsuccessfully attempts to set up a boarding house for Boston's poor children of color, and travels to Jamaica as a missionary. Based on her narrative, Prince did not have any biological children.

Amanda Berry Smith was born to enslaved parents in 1837 in Maryland. Smith's father bought his own freedom after toiling away working toward the goal of freeing his family, and eventually he bought the freedom of his wife and three children when Smith was very young, so young that she knew "nothing about the experience of slavery; because [she] was too young to have any trials of it" (22). Smith began working as a domestic at the age of 13, and she joined the Methodist church. She married her first husband four years later, and continued working as a domestic. After her first husband died in the Civil War, she remarried, and when he died, she became a traveling evangelist. In the 1890s, she found the first orphanage in Illinois for black children. Smith had five children, and only one survived into adulthood. She also adopted two African children during her travels and ministries to Africa.

Susie King Taylor was born "under the slave law in Georgia" in 1848 and was raised by her resourceful grandmother. Though Taylor writes about her brief experience as an enslaved person, her narrative focuses on her experiences as a teacher, nurse, and laundress with the Union Army. Taylor intentionally presents her narratives as a historical account of her noble service to the Union in addition to extolling the black soldiers who fought for freedom, including her first husband, who died in the War. Taylor is a widow when she gives birth to her only son, who dies before Taylor composes her memoir.

As "free" blacks, Prince, Smith, and Taylor were able to find employment though they all performed exploitive and burdensome work in addition to the unpaid labor of family work. Discussing both types of work is fruitful for understanding these women:

"Since work and family have rarely functioned as dichotomous spheres for women of color," according to Collins, "examining racial ethnic women's experiences reveals how these two spheres actually are interwoven" ("Shifting" 46). Indeed, Collins was one of the first black feminist scholars to trouble the private/public distinction as an analytical tool to explain the lives of nineteenth-century woman; the importance of "work" to black mothers is evident because as Evelyn Nakano Glynn notes, women of color "were incorporated into the United States largely to take advantage of their labor," and "there was little interest in preserving family life" (5). Collins' extensive scholarship on the relationship between work and black women's oppression advances feminist analysis of black mothering. Collins has recognized that particularly for women of color, "work is a contested construct and that evaluating individual worth by the type of work performed is a questionable practice in systems based on race and gender inequality" (*Black Feminist Thought* 48). Nonetheless, changes in the organization of work provided the basis of the new (white) maternal ideal. As industrialization took hold in North America, "work" was redefined as entrepreneurship and wage earning, and tied to the cash economy. Men went outside the home to "work," while women remained at home, in "woman's sphere," to rear children.

The idea of woman's sphere—and the equating of maternal presence with "good" mothering—was not only new to the nineteenth century; it was also specific to middle-class culture. Slave mothers, for example, could not possibly exhibit the hallmarks of "good" Victorian mothering. Slave owners forced pregnant and nursing women to work long hours in the field, unable to protect their children, who were, after all, the property of the slave owner. Although, slave owners exploited women's domestic and maternal labor for the use of their own families, slave children could count on the entire black community for everyday care, according to many scholars, including Collins.

Simultaneously, black women's occupation as that of a "Mammy" romanticized the "mothering" skills of some black women—as long as these skills were directed to white children. Although the proslavery apologists declared black women to be lacking in maternal feelings for their own children, they sentimentalized Mammy, who was always there to protect and care for her young white charges. In so doing, they reinforced both the slave system and the gender hierarchy. Therefore, Collins' analysis on black motherhood provides a powerful intervention in articulating and advocating a self-defined analysis of motherhood.

As Collins notes, most black women since the nineteenth century have worked in domestic jobs in both southern and northern cities, and domestic workers "were economically exploited even under the best of circumstances" (*Black Feminist Thought* 56). For most black workers, racism created a daily struggle for survival as blacks faced the challenges of hostility, low-paying jobs, and affordable housing. For example, Nancy Prince, early in her narrative, conveys the extremity of her family's financially unstable reality. Prince's mother remarries twice and has, after Prince's father dies when she is only three months old, several more children. After the second stepfather dies, each family member must work, whether or not they are small children or teenagers:

> There were seven in the family, one sick with a fever, and another in a consumption; and of course, the work must have been very severe, especially the washings. Sabbath evening I had to prepare for the wash; soap the clothes and put them into a steamer, set the kettle of water to boiling, and then closes in the steam, and let the pipe from the boiler into the steam box that held the clothes. At two o'clock, on the morning of Monday, the bell was rung for me to get up; but, that was not all, they said I was too slow, and the washing was not well; I had to leave the tub to tend

> the door and wait on the family, and was not spoken kind to, at that. (Prince 11)

The physical demands of washday, coupled with duties as a housemaid and nursemaid, do not even allow time for sleep. Despite her hard work, the prominent family she works for verbally abuses Prince to try to attempt to emphasize and stress her inferior status and further exaggerate her alienation from the comforts and privileges of middle-class domesticity. Prince's account emphasizes the unrelenting labor involved in maintaining white domesticity, and highlights the dependence of this domesticity on the low-paid labor of servants like her. Besides working as a servant, Prince also finds employment for her numerous brothers and sisters throughout different parts of Massachusetts to experience the kind of abuse and overwork that she does.

Rather than dredging up the most sordid and crushing details of working black womanhood in antebellum New England, Prince is subtle; with a few choice words she manages to describe New England Christians: "I often looked at my employers, and thought to myself, is this your religion? I did not wonder that the girl who had lived there previous to myself, went home to die. They had family prayers, morning and evening. Oh! yes, they were sanctimonious!" (7). This characterization anticipates the critique of New England Christians regarding their "free" brethren in Harriet Wilson's *Our Nig* (1859), a fictionalized autobiography about a free mulatta born and raised in the North, who has little choice but to do physically-debilitating household labor in the home of a Christian family.

When Prince writes, "Hard labor and unkindness was too much for me; in three months, my health and strength were gone," it strengthens the case that it isn't the work that is inferior but how her employers see her work. Indeed, a dignified reticence permeates her narrative, which is poignantly illustrated when she writes, "Soon as the war was over, I determined to get more for my labor" (5). Nancy Prince's narrative is emblematic of how black women's unpaid family labor is simultaneously confining and empowering for black women; as Collins notes, "the theme of how hard black women work is often overlooked" (*Black Feminist Thought* 46).

According to Collins, "Black women wanted to withdraw from the labor force, not to mimic middle-class White women's domesticity but rather, to strengthen the political and economic positions of their families" (*Black Feminist Thought* 54).

Nonetheless, the labor of family work is also disempowering. When Prince writes, "Care after care oppressed me—my mother wandered about like a Jew—the young children who were in families were dissatisfied" (12), we see Prince at the end of her rope. Prince description of her mother as "wandering about like a Jew," denotes an aimless sense of direction while Prince's body is always moving with purpose, and she is always on a mission, whether it is seeking work or family members. Prince's description of her mother challenges the notion of biological motherhood as woman's primary role.

The work of keeping family together and finding them homes and jobs exemplifies Prince as "othermother" and yet it also provides a space for Prince to change her life course, and so she hires "a horse and chaise and took [her mother and sister] both back to Salem, and returned to my place in 1822, with a *determination to do something for myself*; I left my place after three months, and went to learn a trade; and after seven years of anxiety and toil, I made up my mind to leave my country" (15). It is in the next sentence after this declaration that Prince abruptly mentions the arrival of "Mr. Prince," who served in the Russian court, and her marriage to him in terse, diary-like prose: "September 1st, 1823, Mr. Prince arrived from Russia. February 15, 1824, we were married. April 14, we embarked on board the Romulus, captain Epes Sargent commander, bound for Russia" (15). On a practical level, Prince's marriage ensures the way for her to leave the oppressive Northeast to head to Russia where Mr. Prince would return to work. Her exclusion from the comforts and security of middle-class domesticity makes the decision to travel an easy one as it offers her a way to re-imagine black womanhood in order to highlight independence and self-control and claim a maternal femininity at the same time that she pushes the boundaries of gender and race.

Once in St. Petersburg, Prince pursues the entrepreneurial ventures that she could not undertake in America. Prince's first enterprise, taking children to board, begins just three weeks after she arrives.

Prince then realizes that "baby linen making and children's' garments were in great demand" and starts her own business (32). Her enterprise quickly expands and she hires a "journeywoman and apprentices" and even attracts the empress as a customer. Moreover, the support of the Empress emphasizes the difference between attitudes toward black economic activity in the United States and in Russia. Thus, her achievement in Russia connects American racism with the lack of economic opportunity and advancement for free blacks like Prince.

Prince finds confirmation of her maternal identity in her transatlantic travels to Russia. In Russia, though she seems to have easy access to the court of the czar and reports on the fashions and entertainments of that society, Prince makes it clear that she does not gamble or dance. Most of her stay in Russia, she writes, "was taken up in domestic affairs" and in attending Protestant services "twice every Sabbath, and evening prayer meeting, also a female society, so that I was occupied at all times" (32). She takes in children boarders, whom she considers "my family," and though she does not write much about her relationship with them, it is clear that her life in Russia is defined by caretaking and includes work such as making baby clothes and children's garments. Sandra Gunning describes Prince's entrepreneurial work as emblematic of Prince's "new vision of herself as a respected maternal figure" in Russia, one distinct from the life she led in America. This fact underscores the intersection of work, family and black women's oppression, and highlights the dialectical relationship of black women's relationship to work Collins' scholarship has addressed.

When Prince returns from Russia because of her health in 1833, "having been absent about nine years and six months" her goal centers on the well-being of children in Boston, "whose circumstances were similar to my own" (46). Discovering that there were too many black orphans denied shelter "on account of color," Prince is determined to do something: "At this my heart was moved, and I proposed to my friend the necessity of a home for such, where they might be sheltered from the contaminating evils that beset their path" (ibid). Prince is not only concerned about physical shelter for these children, but also concerned about the moral shelter from "evils that beset their path," which recalls the experience of Prince's sister's Sylvia being deluded to a brothel. Unfortunately, Prince is unable to secure funds for the project, but she doesn't give up, saying, "that something must be done for the elevation of the children, and it is for that I labor" (51).

Though Prince may have been subtle about inviting readers to consider race, gender, and class as categories of analysis in terms of reading her narrative, Amanda Berry was more explicit, including "the colored evangelist" in her title. Smith, more extensively than Prince, documents the economic, social, and psychological hardships of growing up black in nineteenth-century America. In her autobiography, Smith writes about the obstacles her family faced as free blacks, records her difficulties having enough money to support her family, and provides many examples of the racism she faced within evangelical circles and when traveling in America and abroad. Because of the sexism and racism Smith encountered, it would have been easy for her to allow controlling stereotypical images of black women do define her existence. Collins' statement that, "In the absence of a viable black feminism that investigates how intersecting oppressions of race, gender, and class foster these contradictions, the angle of vision created by being deemed devalued workers and failed mothers could easily be turned inward, leading to internalized oppression" (*Black Feminist Thought* 11-12) can be easily applied to Smith's life. Because stereotypical images of black women, "as part of a generalized ideology of domination," assume heightened meaning, a nineteenth-century black woman writing her own autobiography is all the more important for articulating a self-defined standpoint amidst racism, sexism, and classism.

Like Prince, Smith's paid labors inevitably intersect with her family obligations.

In her narrative, Smith writes that her poverty-stricken situation frequently forced her to board her daughter, Mazie, in various homes, and "sometimes she was well taken care of and at other times she was not, and when I would go and see the condition of my poor child, and then had to turn away and leave her and go to my work I often cried and prayed; but what could I do more?" (57). Later in the narrative, Smith details the deaths of her children, which often happen while Smith is performing burdensome work:

> I had to do all the cooking for the house, and eight farm hands, beside helping with the washing and doing up all the shirts and fine clothes and looking after my children.... My baby [Nell] seemed to get along nicely for the first three weeks, then she was taken sick with a summer complaint, and in six weeks I had to lay her away in the grave to wait the morning of the Resurrection. (59-60)

Smith records pages and pages of backbreaking work alongside the deaths of her children. After describing about the tragic death of another child, an infant son named Tom Henry, Smith writes:

> I still went on with my washing. Many nights I have stood at my washtub all night, from six in the morning till six the next morning, and so at my ironing table, night and day. I would get so sleepy I could hardly stand on my feet, then I would lean my head on the window ledge and sleep a little till the first deep sleep would pass off, then I would work on till daylight with perfect ease...I worked hard day and night, did all I could to help my husband, but he was one of those poor unfortunate dispositions that are hard to satisfy, and many a day and night m poor heart ached and I wept and prayed God to help me. (68)

Though Smith experiences many trials as "bloodmother," that is, as a biological mother, her biological mothering informs her community othermothering as an evangelist to her spiritual children. Through the death of another son, Will, "the most promising of all the five children I had had" (122), Smith eventually connects her biological mothering to her community othermothering, representing a dynamic life of spiritual leadership and community. Rosetta Haynes describes Smith as a "radical spiritual mother" who "comes to a new understanding of her relationship to divine power" after the death of her favorite son (80). In her narrative, Smith is able to craft a maternal identity designed to empower her though it is important to remember that Smith includes many anecdotes in her narrative that illustrate the oppression black mothers experience.

Though Susie King Taylor's narrative does not record tale after tale of racism and sexism like Smith's autobiography, Taylor as "outraged mother" decries the inhuman treatment against her fellow African Americans by documenting the contributions that members of her race made in the war for freedom. Using the term "outraged mother" to describe Taylor and other nineteenth-century black female autobiographers, Joanne Braxton defines "the outraged mother archetype," as one that relies on a self-sacrificial and nurturing persona to establish moral authority and argues that Taylor "attempts to move public sentiment against the practices of white supremacy that replaced slavery in the South following Reconstruction" (48); these "attempts" exemplify the concept of motherwork. Collins states that, "Black women's motherwork reflects how political consciousness can emerge with every day lived experiences. In this case, Black women's participation in a constellation of mothering activities, collectively called motherwork, often fostered a distinctive political sensibility" (*Black Feminist Thought* 209).

Taylor wrote and published her memoir at the turn-of-the century, often called the nadir of American race relations because of the extreme rise in racial violence, disenfranchisement of blacks, and the legal sanction of Jim Crow, forty years after the end of the Civil War. Taylor proudly reports of her service to the Union as well as the service of the black soldiers who seem to have been forgotten:

> ...so I now present these reminiscences to you, hoping they may prove of some interest, and show how much service and good we can do for each other, and what sacrifices we can make for our liberty and rights, and that there were "loyal women," as well as men, in those days, who did not feel shell or shot, who cared for the sick and dying; women who camped and fared as the boys did, who are still caring for the comrades in their declining years. (v)

Taylor repeats these sentiments throughout her narrative, and it is important to note that her work belongs to the genre of memoir rather than autobiography. I make this distinction because criticism on Taylor focuses on the lack of details of Taylor's "private" life.

As Anthony Barthelemy notes, "we really know little of Susie King Taylor's life...years slip away unrecorded; provocative statement receive no clarification or elaboration" (xliv). I surmise that if we look at the text as a memoir, as a mode of autobiographical writing that "directs attention more toward the lives and actions of others than to the narrator," Taylor's text can be appreciated for it's perceived lack of forthcomingness (Smith and Watson 274). Additionally, if we turn to Collins' work on black women's relationship with the power of self-definition, Taylor's work is invaluable: "For U.S. black women, constructed knowledge of self emerges from the struggle to replace controlling images with self-defined knowledge deemed personally important, usually knowledge essential to black women's survival" (100). As such, Taylor establishes a public embodiment of this knowledge. Believing the work she performed during the Civil War was invaluable, and not simply drudgery, Taylor attempted to support herself by her own literary endeavors.

Taylor not only believes that the nation she proudly served abandoned its financial obligations, she also criticizes the nation for neglecting its legal and moral obligation to protect its black citizens. Writing her narrative is a manifestation of her othermothering responsibilities. Toward the end of her narrative, Taylor writes the following:

> In this "land of free" we are burned, tortured, and denied a fair trial, murdered for any imaginary wrong conceived in the brain of the negro- hating white man. There is no redress from a government, which promised to protect all from under its flag. It seems a mystery to me. They say, "One flag, one nation, one country indivisible." Is this true? Can we say this truthfully, when one race is allowed to burn, hang, and inflict the most horrible torture weekly, monthly, on another? No, we cannot sing, "My country, t'is of thee, Sweet land of Liberty"! It is hollow mockery. (62)

Taylor repeats this refrain in her last chapter, "A Visit to Louisiana" where she reports her trip to Shreveport, Louisiana from

Boston in order to nurse her dying son. Here, she uses the example of her inability to bring him home to die to further her case of racial injustice and links him to war: "It seemed very hard, when his father fought to protect the Union and our flag, and yet his boy was denied, under this same flag, a berth to carry him home to die, because he was a negro" (72).

CONCLUSION

The autobiographical texts by Nancy Prince, Amanda Berry Smith, and Susie King Taylor introduce us to three othermothers of nineteenth-century America, whose unshakable maternal authority and authenticity transformed their lives and the lives of others. The concept of motherwork, uniquely articulated in their life stories, provides a productive way to inform our study of the lives and texts of nineteenth-century black women. Although motherwork is focused on the concepts of mothering, it reaches beyond women who are biologically mothers, as embodied in the term "othermothers." As a tool for resistance and social justice, motherwork and othermothering provides a mechanism for the survival of black women and the survival of their communities because it is an active effort to confront oppression with the goal of advancing the concerns of black women, children, and men.

Nancy Prince expresses what this type of maternal work means for her and her family, and in writing her narrative, Prince affirms her desire to contribute to the survival of her community. Amanda Berry Smith wrote her autobiography with the belief that her record helping others according to Christian doctrine would lead others to lead a Christian life; she becomes a spiritual mother to those seeking spiritual guidance. Susie King Taylor articulates her political position and demands on behalf of the black men who fought for the nation in the Civil War. As "outraged mother," in the words of Joanne Braxton, Taylor attends to motherwork by addressing the unique complications women of color face when deconstructing systems of racism and patriarchy. An in-depth consideration of these writings, using the theories of Patricia Hill Collins, sheds new light on the articulations of mothering that emerge from their autobiographical texts and links their kind of motherwork to contemporary black feminist theory, highlighting a strong tradition of black feminist thought.

WORKS CITED

Barthelemy, Anthony G. "Introduction." *Collected Black Women's Narratives*. Nancy Prince, Rev. H. Mattison, A. M. Bethany Veney and Susie King Taylor. New York: Oxford University Press, 1988. xxix-xlviii.

Berger, Aimee E. "The Voice of the Maternal in Louise Erdich's Fiction and Memoirs." *Feminist Mothering*. Ed. Andrea O'Reilly. Albany: State University of New York Press, 2008. 89-106.

Braxton, Joanne. *Black Women Writing Autobiography: A Tradition Within a Tradition*. Philadelphia: Temple University Press, 1989.

Collins, Patricia Hill. "Shifting the Center: Race, Class, and Feminist Theorizing about Motherhood." *Mothering: Ideology, Experiencing and Agency*. Ed. Evelyn Nakano Glenn, Grace Chang, and Linda Forcey. New York: Routledge, 1994. 45-65.

Collins, Patricia Hill. *Black Feminist Thought: Knowledge, Consciousness, and the Politics of Empowerment*. 2nd ed. New York: Routledge, 1998.

Daly, Brendy O., and Maureen T. Reddy, eds. *Narrating Mother: Theorizing Maternal Subjectivities*. Knoxville: University of Tennessee Press, 1991.

Ducille, Ann. "On Canons: Anxious History and the Rise of Black Feminist Literary Studies." *The Cambridge Companion to Feminist Literary Theory*. Ed. Ellen Rooney. Cambridge: Cambridge University Press, 2006. 29-52.

Gunning, Sandra. "Nancy Prince and the Politics of Mobility, Home, and Diasporic (Mis)Identification." *American Quarterly* 53 (March 2001): 32-69.

Haynes, Rosetta. *Radical Spiritual Motherhood: Autobiography and Empowerment in Nineteenth-Century African American Women*. Baton Rouge: Louisiana State University Press, 2011.

Kerber, Linda. *Toward an Intellectual History of Women: Essays by Linda Kerber*. Chapel Hill: University of North Carolina Press, 1997.

Kritzer, Amelia Howe. "Playing with Republican Motherhood: Self-Representation in Plays by Susanna Haswell Rowson and Judith Sargent Murray." *Early American Literature* 31.2 (January 1996): 150-66.

Prince, Nancy. *A Black Woman's Odyssey Through Russia and Jamaica: The Narrative of Nancy*. New York: Marcus Wiener Publishing, 1990.

Smith, Amanda Berry. *An Autobiography: The Story of the Lord's Dealings with Mrs. Amanda Smith the Colored Evangelist*. 1893. New York: Oxford University Press, 1988.

Smith, Sidonie and Julia Watson, eds. *Reading Autobiography: A Guide for Interpreting Life Narratives*. 2nd ed. Minneapolis: University of Minnesota Press, 2010.

Taylor, Susie King. *Reminiscences of My Life in Camp with the 33rd U.S. Colored Troops, Late 1st South Carolina Volunteers*. Boston: Susie King Taylor, 1902.

Situated Knowledge—Coming to Voice, Coming to Power

The Mothers Committee of Bayview Hunters

NANCY ARDEN MCHUGH

DUE TO HIGHER THAN NATIONAL AVERAGE breast cancer rates and deaths on Long Island, the U.S. Congress in 1993 ordered a study of breast cancer on the island. The Long Island Breast Cancer Study Project (LIBCSP), federally funded under Public Law 103-43, conducted by the National Cancer Institute in collaboration with the National Institute of Environmental Health Science, is aimed at investigating environmental causes of breast cancer. The National Cancer Institute states "[t]he LIBCSP consists of more than ten studies that include human population (epidemiologic) studies, the establishment of a family breast and ovarian cancer registry, and laboratory research on mechanisms of action and susceptibility in development of breast cancer." Women on Long Island have long suspected that their breast cancer was linked to various environmental causes, such as pesticide spraying for mosquitoes, municipal waste, and industrial air pollution and water pollution.

On the other side of the country, during the same time period African American women in Bayview Hunters Point, California suspected that their breast cancer and other illness in their community were linked to industrial air pollution, water pollution, municipal waste, and radiation from a local Naval shipyard (Fishman; Allday). A study of these women, conducted from 1987-1993 and published in 1995, also revealed higher than national average rates of breast cancer and deaths in this community (Gills). Yet unlike the women of Long Island, the women of Bayview Hunters Point were not written into a congressionally backed and federally funded research effort that consisted of any studies, let alone ten studies. There is no National Cancer Institute "Bayview Hunters Point Breast Cancer Study Project." How are we to account for the disparities in research priorities and funding? There are two significant demographic differences that differently situate these communities: race and class.

The breast cancer rates from Bayview Hunters Point reflect illness and deaths of African American women who live below the poverty line, where as the women of Long Island are, by in large, white and affluent. The failure of the government to fund a study akin to the Long Island study is even more worrisome considering that African American women are more likely to die from breast cancer than white women. The National Cancer Institute reported 33.5 deaths per 100,000 for Black women compared to 24.4 deaths per 100,000 for white women. In the case of Long Island, the death rate for the two counties of concern, Nassau and Suffolk, was 28.0 and 29.0 per 100,000, which is higher than the national average, but not higher than the mortality rate for Black women. My point here is not to denigrate the efforts of Long Island activists, but to question why these women were able to get support for a federally funded study while the illness and deaths of the women of Bayview Hunters Point goes unnoticed? Race and class not only positioned the Long Island women within a valorized social location, in that, they had resources to make themselves heard, and they were also able to make their lives and deaths more noticeable. Patricia Hill Collins, in her book *Fighting Words*, describes this lack of recognition of the health needs of these Black women were the result of the politics of containment, where these women's physical location tied to their race and class "contained" them such that they go unnoticed. In spite of their "containment," the women of Bayview Hunters Point refused to let their health, community and lives go unnoticed. They resisted. Because of the multiple and intersecting levels of oppression, the women of Bayview Hunters Point had to develop alternative resources, methods, and coalitions through which to be heard. This essay is as much the story about how they go about resisting oppression, being heard and affecting change, as it is an argument about the efficacy of situated knowledge and the epistemic importance of coalition building.

In this essay, I use the experiences and activism of the women of Bayview Hunters Point (BVHP), focusing specifically on a community action group called the Mothers Committee, to develop arguments for situated knowledge, and to point to the trajectory that I see these arguments taking—that of "increasingly concrete engagements" (Tsing 267). I argue that situation is a vital epistemic location that is salient to its members, it is a place to know, and it is a place from which to initiate transformative practices, as well as a place that is transformed. Situation has the potential to generate different possibilities for community knowledge and thus for creating change.

In addition to the Bayview Hunters Point and the Mothers Committee function as worthy examples of situated knowledge, because provide a critical example of environmental, health, and racial injustice, and how these same communities resist injustice. Thus, the equally important goal of this essay is to highlight just how this community is subjected to, experiences, and resists injustice. Finally, my goal in this essay is not to critically assess the merits of arguments for situated knowledge. Instead it is to employ them in order to understand their potential to help us to "rearrange and reconstruct in some way, be it little or large, the world in which we live" (Dewey 138). My goal is thus a pragmatic one. It is, in a sense, an employed response to the question that Janet Kournay raises in "The Place of Standpoint Theory in Feminist Science Studies" "is standpoint theory [and other situated approaches] a resource" for feminist science studies, and I would add, for social change (209)?

LOCATING THE MOTHERS COMMITTEE

Excerpt from *The San Francisco Chronicle,* Monday, May 15, 2006:

> "Big victory for Hunters Point activists"
> The 77-year-old Pacific Gas and Electric Co. power plant on Evans Avenue officially closes today. People who live in public housing directly across the street and other homes nearby began organizing more than 25 years ago—with protests, lawsuits and countless meetings—to rid their

> neighborhood of what came to represent the area's disproportionate share of San Francisco's heavy industry, and of the city's asthma and cancer cases. "To say the least, I am elated," said Marie Harrison, a member of the Huntersview Mothers Committee who got involved a decade ago, after realizing that lung-clogging particulate matter from the plant was drifting through her grandson's bedroom windows. "Our children have suffered chronic nosebleeds and asthma attacks as a result of that plant." I am giddy, like a little kid, that we got that monster out of our community. "Most significant, said resident Tessie Ester, was that the kids could be outside jumping rope and playing football and that, even with a strong breeze, she could be certain they weren't inhaling fumes from the power plant. "The smoke has stopped," Ester said. "When I look over at those stacks, and there is nothing coming out, I can't help but cry. We should never have been forced to live like that. Maybe now we can get rid of the inhalers and really start to enjoy life." (A-1)

The Bayview Hunters Point Mothers Environmental Health and Justice Committee, aka, the Mothers Committee, is a "grassroots community group," a citizens-science group, that was formed by the Huntersview Tenants Association and the Greenaction for Health and Environmental Justice in San Francisco (2). The purpose of the group is to "mobilize, train, and empower community mothers in the fight for environmental health and justice in Bayview Hunters Point" (2). Greenaction[1] helped to train the members of the Mothers Committee in computer, research, media and public speaking skills. The organization also trained members in environmental health, community organizing, and how to work with government organizations (2). Over the course of a year, 2002-2003, "they collected information about their community, attended and spoke at government information meetings and hearings, and visited government agencies and met with government officials to advocate for their community" (2). From these activities in 2004 they generated the report "Pollution, Health, Environmental Racism and Injustice: A Toxic Inventory of Bayview Hunters Point, San

Francisco." The report compiles and assesses information about the Bayview Hunters Point environment, the businesses that impact its environment, and the health of the members of the community. From this assessment, the Committee also presented a series of recommendations and steps for future work.

The EPA considers the Bayview Hunters Point (BVHP) neighborhood in San Francisco to be one of the most chemically contaminated communities in the U.S. and "over half of the land in San Francisco that is zoned for industrial use is in Bayview Hunters Point" (Mothers Committee 3). The most impacted part of this neighborhood is the community of 12,000 residents that live on the east side of Third Street, where the homes of the Mothers Committee members are located (Mothers Committee 5). Seventy percent of this community is African American, 15 percent Asian (consisting largely of Chinese and Pacific Islanders), and the final 15 percent either Caucasian or Hispanic. Forty percent or more of the people live at subsistence level incomes (Mothers Committee 5). This community was also home to the PG&E power plant for 77 years until the Mothers Committee helped force its closure in 2006 (Fulbright A-1). In addition to this, Bayview Hunters Point is also the location of a federal EPA superfund site, the now abandoned Hunters Point Naval Shipyard, as well as "a sewage treatment plant that handles 80 percent of the City's solid waste, 100 Brownfield sites (a Brownfield is an abandoned, idle, or underused industrial or commercial facility where expansion or redevelopment is limited because of environmental contamination), 187 leaking underground tanks (LUFTS), and more than 124 hazardous waste handlers regulated by the USEPA" (Mothers Committee 5). The EPA states that Bayview Hunters Point is home to more than 200 toxic chemicals and materials.

According to Mitchell H. Katz, M.D., in "Health Programs in Bayview Hunters Points and Recommendations for Improving the Health of Bayview Hunter's Point Residents" Bayview Hunters Point is also home to a disproportionately high number of sick people. There is a high rate of asthma among children, a high rate of birth defects and infant mortality (Katz 18), and one of the highest rates of breast cancer in the country (Fishman; Allday). This last fact is significant because African American women are statistically less likely to contract breast cancer than white women and the women in this community are getting breast cancer younger and of a more deadly type (National Cancer Institute SEER).

THE METHODOLOGIES OF *THIS* OPPRESSED GROUP

The view that all knowers and knowledge are situated is one of the most important and tangible insights generated in feminist science studies. It has resulted in epistemological and methodological reframings of scientific practices, and has led to ongoing critical work in feminist science studies and feminist epistemology. Although Donna Haraway was the first to use the term "situated knowledge" in her 1988 essay "Situated Knowledge: The Science Question in Feminism and the Privilege of Partial Perspective," it has been developed more fully in feminist philosophy of science in recent years by such writers as Sandra Harding and Lorraine Code, and has been enhanced by work outside of science studies by feminist theorists such as Patricia Hill Collins, Sarah Hoagland, Chandra Mohanty, and Chela Sandoval. At its most basic level, all knowledge is situated and all knowledge is generated from a knower's particular location, which consists of the complex unfolding resulting from one's social, material, epistemological, gendered, lived bodily experience. Yet, as Collins points out situated knowledge reflects knowledge that arises from collective experiences, not isolated knowers (*Fighting Words*). Situated knowledge and standpoint theorists understand that what is epistemically significant about situated knowledge is that it initiates from located experience and also necessarily from the work of gaining a learned, critical perspective. As Harding articulates in her 2008 *Sciences from Below: Feminisms, Postcolonialities, and Modernities*, "all understanding is socially local, or situated" (120). But this is not sufficient for developing a standpoint epistemology or situated knowledge. Instead standpoint is an "achievement, not an ascription" (120). One does not acquire such an epistemic view only as the result of oppression, but instead it is a "group achievement" that develops as a result of collective critical inquiry and critical dialogue that raises questions about "dominant institutions" and practices (Harding 120).

In *Methodology of the Oppressed* Chela Sandoval distils Haraway's arguments by developing its methodological significance, also emphasizing the work required to achieve a critical standpoint. Though standpoint theory and situated knowledge positions have been employed in a dual role as methodology and epistemology, or as Harding describes are "two sides of a coin" (*Sciences from Below* 193) since their inception, Sandoval does particularly important work in emphasizing the methodological import of these epistemologies. In doing so she moves this work in a direction that recognizes the seamless relationship between knowing and doing. Sandoval argues that when one works from an "oppositional consciousness" or a situated knowledge position, she is necessarily employing the methodology of the oppressed (175). Employing the experience of subjugation, or learning to see and know from the perspective of the oppressed creates transformative engagements with the world. The act of working to locate, articulate, and critique one's own subject position when one is oppressed and then critically engaging the world from this perspective to create change is an unexpected methodology for people who have been subjugated. Sandoval argues that "[i]t has been assumed that the oppressed will behave without recourse to any *particular* method, or rather, that their behavior consists of whatever acts one must commit in order to survive, whether physically or psychically" (176). In other words, those with power assume, that the only way that those that are subjugated can act is merely by brute reaction to what they are faced with immediately. Sandoval argues that, in fact, the oppressed can develop a methodology through a critical framing of their epistemic location and this position can be strategic because of its situated nature. This insight is important because it requires that we see actions of oppressed groups as grounded, knowledge infused, intentional engagements with the world, instead of as the random acts of desperation; Situated knowledge as the "methodology of the oppressed can now be recognized as the mode of being best suited to life under" globalization (176). Collins makes a similar point, arguing that Black women have employed what she calls "visionary pragmatism" as a means to resist under conditions of oppression (189). Visionary pragmatism emphasizes the importance of "struggling for an ethical end" over "arriving at a predetermined destination" and connects this ethical end to part of a broader struggle (189-190). This requires a particular strategic way of acting given one's conditions and particular ability to be able to envision how seemingly small outcomes are part of a larger and perhaps more abstract goal.

The Mothers Committee of BVHP provides a pertinent example of members of an oppressed group working strategically to change their living conditions. Members of the Huntersview Tenants Association were well aware that they were living in an environment that was unhealthy. Because they realized that they needed to work strategically, they formed a working relation with Greenaction for Environmental Health and Justice, an organization with access to information that could provide the Tenants Association with the skills and knowledge to change their community. Thus, the Tenants Association's first strategy was coalition building with a like-minded, differently situated group, Greenaction, which had connections and resources that BVHP community members needed. The Tenants Association was able to recognize that there were gaps in their knowledge that could best be filled through this relationship, just as Greenaction was able to recognize that there were gaps in their knowledge about BVHP that could be filled by those that were inside the community. Neither group had all of the knowledge or skills needed to create change in BVHP, but each was able to recognize the epistemic and methodological gains that could be had from working together. Thus, from this relationship Bayview Mothers Environmental Health and Justice Committee (The Mothers Committee) was formed. With Greenaction and the Mothers Committee now collaborating the members of the Mothers Committee were able to recruit and train people from their community. They obtained grant funding, gathered and assessed scientific information about their local environment, local disease rates, health outcomes, as well as population statistics and information about businesses and industry in their community. With these resources in hand they developed a comprehensive and persuasive set of data that provided a "toxic inventory" of BVHP. "Toxic inventory" is a term normally used by governmental and scientific organizations such as the Environmental Protection Agency or the Regional Air Pollution Control Agency to describe inventories of "chemicals released to ... water, air and land" in order to conduct toxic risk assessments, assessments of the likelihood of a chemical causing disease or death (EPA History).

Through coalition building, the Mothers Committee self-consciously learned and utilized the terminology, methods, and resources most likely to convince those with power to listen and act. With the assistance of Greenaction, they were trained in and used standard research methods, methods that most people assume are outside the reach of a marginalized community, to effect change. With solid data in hand and the ability to make themselves heard and listened to they were able to achieve one of their primary goals—"organizing the community to close the PG&E Hunters Point Power Plant" (Mothers Committee 30). To reiterate Sandoval and Collins' points in terms of the Mothers Committee, they behaved *with* recourse to particular methods and did so such that they would survive physically and psychically. The Mothers Committee recognized that their experience in BVHP didn't accord with what they knew their lives should be like. This led them to seek out information and build relationships with differently situated groups. The differently situated knowledge of both groups helped the other see the gaps in their knowledge and develop a critical understanding of their needs and critical strategies for addressing the needs. Thus, what can be known when the Mothers Committee and Greenaction work together exceeds what any one groups could know on its own. Thus, the methodology of this oppressed group was strategically oriented for the survival of their community on multiple levels, including the ability and means to methodologically, epistemologically and technologically build knowledge to effect change.

THE MOTHERS COMMITTEE "COMING TO VOICE, COMING TO POWER"

Collins argues that "[f]or Black women as a collectivity, emancipation, liberation, or empowerment as a group rests on two interrelated goals" (*Fighting Words* 45). These are the power and significance that comes from self-defining and the right to determine one's own future and goals. The Mothers Committee reflects the importance of "coming to voice, coming to power" through self-definition and self-determination and how doing so frames knowing and doing. The members of the Mothers Committee of Bayview Hunters Point self-consciously utilized their oppositional positioning to their advantage as part of their methodology as an oppressed group. It is no accident that there are groups like the "Mothers Committee." Like many women's groups, such as Mothers Against Drunk Drivers or Mothers of the Disappeared in Argentina, they clearly define and center their group's identity and interests on gender and the care and stewardship of their community. Just as mothers in many parts of the world are responsible for the health, care, and well-being of their community and surroundings, the Mothers Committee embraces this as an instrumental part of their identity; they unite around it, and use it to guide what they know and what they can and should do.

From their perspective as mothers and stewards of their community, they have seen that their "children have suffered chronic nosebleeds and asthma attacks;" they have experienced the high rates of breast cancer and birth defects; they know what is like to keep their windows shut for fear of their children are inhaling particulates from local industry. They know their environment is toxic because they live in it and have to care for others that live in it (Mothers Committee 6). And this knowledge about their community is accurate. In the 2006 "Health Programs in Bayview Hunters Point and Recommendations for Improving Health" it was reported that 10 percent of the community had asthma; 15.5 percent of the children had asthma. The asthma rate for the general U.S. population is 5.6 percent (8). The rate of birth defects in the area was "44.3 per 1000, compared to 33.1 per 1000 births for the rest of San Francisco County" (Mothers Committee 6). The breast cancer rate is double that of the rest of San Francisco and one of the highest in the country (Mothers Committee 6; Allday). Furthermore, they know that breast cancer studies that only look at threshold levels, studies of individual chemicals and their individual toxicity to humans, and claim that the particular chemicals in their community cannot cause cancer are not accounting for the complexity of their lives in which they live with multiple chemicals over long periods of time. As one community member stated: "the standards that [scientists are] using, measuring, environmental studies are not based on reality. They are based on laboratory needs and economics. Therefore, there isn't an appropriate instrument to use to study this phenomenon we're addressing" (Fishman 197). They know because of how they have worked to be critically situated.

Although many early arguments, such as Harding's and Haraway's, for situated knowledge grounded their arguments in the lives of women, they did so in a way that is distanced from the lives of actual women and their material location.[2] Chandra Mohanty in *Feminism without Borders: Decolonizing theory, practicing solidarity* is explicit in formulating epistemological positions that allow us to consider how physical location and global capitalism merge to create particularized systems of knowledge that also reflect some common interests of women in general. Mohanty points to the "bodies and lives of women and girls from the ...Two-Thirds World," arguing that, "global capitalism writes its script" on these bodies (234). If we attend to and theorize about the experiences of these women and girls, we are able to take apart global capitalism, recognizing its inherent racism, sexism, and classism, and engage in anti-capitalist resistance. In "The Project of Feminist Epistemology: A Non Western Feminist on Epistemology" Uma Narayan rightly points out that feminists need to engage the "methodological habit" of situating the experiences of oppressed women in their "historical and cultural settings" yet avoid making "comparisons across such settings, given the dangers of attempting to compare what may well be incomparable in any neat terms" (260). White U.S. feminists in philosophy of science worked to take the kind of criticisms made by Narayan, Collins, and Mohanty to heart. This can especially be seen in Harding's work.

This attention of moving between the particular and the collective becomes well articulated in Sandra Harding's *Science and Social Inequality: Feminist and Post-Colonial Issues,* a sustained analysis of global injustice and science. Perhaps in a desire to be more explicit about the methodological components of her argument, Harding begins to describe standpoint epistemology, as a situated knowledge position. Unlike earlier feminist arguments in philosophy of science that tended to situate women in homogenized categories, Harding's newer arguments for situated knowledge move between the particular and the collective while rejecting the epistemological individualism in mainstream epistemology and science studies. By drawing on the work of feminist ethnoscientists such as Vandana Shiva, and feminists working on gender and development, such as Rosi Bradiotti and Drucilla Barker, Harding develops a critically grounded standpoint epistemology. This represents an important move in feminist science studies because as she begins to think about "women collectively, in their culturally particular social situations," she formulates a dynamic and concrete conception of knowledge generated by women in and about the situations in which they live (99). Harding argues that the ethnoscience movement has pointed overtly to the different ways women's standpoints are generated in gendered cultures and particularized by their interactions with "with local natural and social environments'" (99). Women's experiences, standpoints, and needs differ based on the material conditions of their lives. Harding points to the most basic aspects of experience, the place which one inhabits and the way gender mediates one's experience of place, to make apparent the concrete nature of situated knowledge and she negotiates the difficult terrain between local and global, emphasizing differences and commonalities in experience and situation. From this she argues that all sciences are "ethnosciences" because the sciences interact with the world based on the locations in which they are developed, the interests they have in the world, the "discursive traditions" they develop, such as "metaphors, models, analogies, and narratives ...used to identify and explain features of the world around them, and finally cultures have their own ways of generating knowledge that are proficient at "detect[ing] some of nature's regularities while obscuring others" (140).

BAYVIEW HUNTERS POINT IS A PLACE TO KNOW

This increased focus on materiality and the concrete nature of situation and its epistemic and methodological importance for science is especially apparent in Lorraine Code's argument for ecological thinking. In *Ecological Thinking: The Politics of Epistemic Location* Code emphasizes the importance of place, as habitat and as an epistemological location. She argues that a significant aspect of situated knowledge is that it is not just a place from which to interrogate and generate knowledge, location—social location and physical location/habitat—is a place to be interrogated. Code views situation or "habitat as a place to know" and emphasizes that, like all living things, humans are ecological subjects (37). Just as ecology must take into account all the interactions an organism engages in, experiences, and is affected by, ecological thinking "builds on the relations of organisms with one another and with their habitat, which comprises not just the physical habitat or the present one, but the complex network of locations and relations, whether social, historical, material, geographical, cultural, racial, sexual, institutional, or other, where organisms—human or non-human—try to live well, singly or collectively" (91). Code's work generates an epistemology from the methodologies in ecology and in turn uses this epistemology to generate a methodological approach to knowing the world. Thus, ecological thinking is a way to know "us," humans, in the world, and provides a fuller accounting and direction for engaging in the world than less situated modes of philosophical practice have provided.

Like many oppressed groups, the community of Bayview Hunters Point live in conditions that are not conducive to living well, conditions that cause and exacerbate illness. As I stated earlier in the chapter, the Mothers Committee points to a number of environmental conditions contributing to the poor health of the community. Whether we think about environment broadly to include the way humans inhabit space and the way space is constructed, or narrowly to merely include air, water, soil quality, with either way of understanding the situation of the Mothers Committee, it is not hard to see how the place they inhabit is unique and how it is a place to know and to know from.[3]

Bordering the neighborhood of the Mothers Committee is an EPA Superfund Site, The Hunters Point Naval Shipyard, which has numerous different types of contaminants; among them are radiological, mercury, lead, methane, and particulate matter (EPA). The Hunters Point Naval Shipyard was established in 1869 and operated through 1991 when the Department of Defense listed it for closure by the Department of Defense (EPA). From the late 1940s through to the late 1970s it was also the site of the National

Radiological Defense Laboratory. In 1989 Hunters Point Naval Shipyard was put on the National Priorities list, thus designating it an EPA Superfund Site (EPA). By 1992 the EPA, the Navy, and the State of California signed a Federal Facilities Agreement to investigate and clean up the shipyard. It was divided into six different sites (A-F) to facilitate clean up. Although many of these sites share borders with the BVHP neighborhood, Parcel E is less than 800 feet from family homes. It is also potentially the most dangerous parcel of land in the shipyard. Parcel E "is a 46-acre industrial landfill which operated from 1958 to 1974. The landfill received liquid chemical waste, asbestos, domestic wastes and refuse, dredge spoil materials, sandblast grit solvent wastes [such as arsenic and lead], and low-level radioactive wastes from shipboard radium dials including electronic equipment" (Agency for Toxic Substances and Disease Registry). Furthermore, housing in this area existed prior to the landfill. So the Navy made a decision to place this landfill near these homes. Thus, the people living in this part of BVHP were doing so in immediate proximity to this landfill. Numerous studies link cancer to low-level radiation exposure (Matanoski et al; Zhou et al; Wing et al.) and many other health conditions, such as lung disease, childhood developmental delay, and birth defects, are linked to exposure to the other materials contained in the landfill (Diawara).

Because of the large amount of industry in the area there is a high level of air pollution: "The Bay Area Air Quality Management District (BAAQMD) estimates that of 39 pollutants they measure in San Francisco neighborhoods, the highest concentration, 20 pollutants, was found in Bayview Hunters Point...." (6). The weather patterns in the Bay Area also contribute to the poor air quality by temperature inversions, which keep air pollutant close to the ground, and seasonal winds that blow "air pollution from industrial operations at the Naval Shipyard, the Mirant Power Plant, and PG&E 's Hunters Point Plant ... back into the community during most of the year...." (6-7).

Social factors contribute to poor health in BVHP. In "Health Programs in Bayview Hunters Point and Recommendations for Improving the Health of Bayview Hunter's Point Residents" Dr. Mitchell H. Katz argues that "BVHP experiences a disproportionate number of social determinants with adverse effects on health, ranging from social isolation to institutional and environmental racism to lack of access to healthy food" (2). Access to healthy food is a serious challenge facing community members. Until 2008 there were no full service grocery stores in the community. A survey launched by the Community Capacity Building Project reported that less than five percent of foods stocked in BVHP stores consisted of fresh produce. The most stocked products were junk food, alcohol, and tobacco (Katz 11). Mark Ghaly, co-chair of the working group and director of the Southeast Health Center stated, "This lack of options contributes to the health problems that plague the area.... If we can get more convenient access to healthy foods, it would make a difference among the citizens I serve at my clinic" (Temple). In December of 2007 it was announced that Tesco, a British grocery chain, would open the first full service grocery store in BVHP.

Violence is the leading cause of shortened life expectancy in BVHP. This obviously is a problem on its own, but it also contributes to the overall stress levels and poor health experienced in the community. Residents report that they don't feel safe walking to neighborhood parks for exercise or to get their children outside (Katz 13). Domestic violence is high in this community, which affects women, children, and the elderly on multiple and significant levels (Katz 10). Furthermore, there is not ready access to healthcare in BVHP. For example, even though the children of Bayview Hunters Point have a disproportionate number of health problems and the community has the "highest density of children, [as of 2006 it still] has only one pediatrician in private practice"(Lelchuk B1). Mitchell H. Katz provides numerous recommendations for improving health services in the community, many of which consist in providing access to basic preventative care. The residents of BVHP are in a situation in which any problems that they experience from their physical environment are exacerbated by their social climate in which they experience racism and don't have access to good food, to medical care, a safe neighborhood, and exercise. All of these factors function transactionally to make BVHP a toxic environment, as the Mothers Committee "Toxic Inventory" report reveals.

The residents of BVHP have an excellent understanding of how their lives and their experiences with disease differ from other groups. As Jennifer Fishman argues in her article on BVHP, risk assessment, and breast cancer, "Assessing Breast Cancer: Risk, Science and Environmental Activism in an 'At Risk' Community,"

> the breast cancer rates in this community run counter to the statistics for the "average" person. The statistically 'average' woman with breast cancer is white, middle-class and post menopausal. In contrast, the "average" woman with breast cancer in BVHP is black, poor, and pre-menopausal. The activists see this contradiction not only as evidence of environmental links to breast cancer in BVHP, but also as evidence of the fact that risk assessment does not, and cannot, acknowledge the different risk factors that might exist for other types of women. (199)

Although this is an earlier and different citizens-science group than the Mothers Committee, Fishman's work illustrates not only how disease is experienced differently in this community, but how the residents use their experience with disease, combined with the scientific knowledge they obtained by working with collaboratively to show how particular scientific methodologies cannot account for illness in their community.

CONCLUSION

The Mothers Committee provided a fuller accounting of the health of their community by using "average" as a place from which to know; they used their lives in this location as an epistemic site. They also viewed "average" as a place to know—they gained the scientific knowledge about their physical surroundings and how they related to the health of their community to construct a convincing argument, and they reflected how their situation and their knowledge of their location is unique and authoritative. They were able to show that they are ecological subjects impacted by their environment in multiple ways. Finally, the Mothers Committee initiated change in their community and pointed to other changes that need to take place for their community to live well.

The work of the Mothers Committee, like Code's, Collins', Harding's, Mohanty's and Sandoval's work, represents the newer formulations of situated knowledge that ethnographer Anna Lowenhaupt Tsing calls "increasingly concrete engagements." In her 2006 book *Friction: An Ethnography of Global Connection,* which is an analysis of the effects of globalization on specific communities in Kalimantan, Indonesia—Tsing describes "concrete engagements" as a self-conscious "research strategy," i.e., a methodology, that creates intervention points and negotiates between the shared and the particular to "encourage critical purchase" (267). This generates the ability to act and effect change. Not only must we critically recognize the material particularities of each situation, we must self-consciously "reach across the world" (267) to recognized how coalitions can be built, just as the Huntersview Tenants Association and Greenaction reached toward the other forming the Mothers Committee and affecting change in Bayview Hunters Point.

Though Tsing's work as an ethnographer differs in many practical ways from the work of Haraway, Sandoval, Collins, Harding, Mohanty, and Code, she does provide a useful analytical and terminological way of thinking about the growth of arguments for situated knowledge. These arguments have moved in the direction of increasingly concrete engagements that recognize situation as a vital epistemic location—a place from which to know and a place to know or interrogate—as well as a place that is socially, materially, and historically salient to its members. Situation is also a methodological location from which to initiate critical, transformative practices, practices that are informed by location. Finally, situation is a place whose conditions are transformed by its own methodology as well as a place that methodologically transforms epistemology.

In 2013, the Mothers Committee is still active. Tessie Ester, mentioned in the news release about the closing down of PG&E Hunter's Power Plant earlier in this essay, serves on the board of directors for Greenaction, as apt location for her critical skills. The Mothers Committee and Greenaction have started a campaign to have the U.S. government take responsibility for fully cleaning up the naval shipyard. They also were able to get PG&E to stop sending its PCB waste from the clean up of the power plant site to Kettleman City in the San Joaquin Valley. This town of mostly farmworkers has a reportedly high rate of birth defects, miscarriages and infant mortality (Greenaction 9/17/13). The Mothers Committee continue "coming to voice, coming to power" to advocate for their community and those similarly situated.

"Situated Knowledge-Coming to Voice, Coming to Power: The Mothers Committee of Bayview Hunters" is based upon work supported by the National Science Foundation under Grant No. 0541512. Any opinions, findings, and conclusions or recommendations expressed in this material are those of the author and do not necessarily reflect the views of the National Science Foundation.

[1]Greenaction's mission is a U.S. organization that works nationally and internationally to "mobilize community power to win victories that change government and corporate policies and practices to protect health and to promote environmental justice."
[2]Gaile Pohlhaus makes a similar point.
[3]One could be concerned that "to know" from a place could lead to confined or narrow vision. In the case of oppressed groups their vision tends to be broader than that of the mainstream. As Patricia Hill Collins and Chela Sandoval articulate, this the needs of survival requires that these groups have an outsider/within perspective, where they are able to know their situation intimately while also knowing that of their oppressors.

WORKS CITED

Allday, Erin. "Breast cancer mortality studied in black women." *San Francisco Chronicle* May 18, 2007. Web. May 22, 2014.

Code, Lorianne. *Ecological Thinking*. Oxford: Oxford University Press, 2006.

Code, Lorianne. *Rhetorical Spaces: Essays on Gendered Locations*. New York: Routledge, 1995.

Code, Lorianne. *What Can She Know?* Ithaca, NY: Cornell University Press, 1991.

Collins, Patricia Hill. *Black Feminist Thought*. 2nd ed. New York: Routledge, 2000.

Collins, Patricia Hill. *Fighting Words*. Minneapolis: University of Minnesota Press, 1998.

Collins, Patricia Hill. "Learning from the Outsider Within." *Social Problems* 33.6 (1998): 14-32.

Dewey, John. *The Quest for Certainty*. New York: Capricorn Books, 1929.

Diawara, Moussa M. et al. "Arsenic, Cadmium, Lead, and Mercury in Surface Soils, Pueblo, Colorado: Implications for Population Health Risk." *Environmental Geochemistry and Health* 28.4 (2006): 297-315. Web. March 2014.

Environmental Protection Agency. Bayview Hunters Point Ship Yard. Web. August 2014

Environmental Protection Agency (EPA). *Health Effects of Radiation*. Web. June 2014.

Environmental Protection Agency (EPA). *History*. Web. June 2014.

Fishman, Jennifer. "Assessing Breast Cancer: Risk, Science and Environmental Activism in an 'At Risk' Community." *Ideologies of Breast Cancer*. Ed. Laura Potts. New York: St. Martins Press, 2000. 181-204.

Fulbright, Laura. "Big victory for Hunters Point activists." *San Francisco Chronicle* May 15, 2006: A-1.

Gillis, Debbie. "Comparison of Incidence of Cancer in Selected Sites Between Bayview/Hunters Point and San Francisco and the Bay Area." Bureau of Epidemiology, Disease Control and AIDS, San Francisco Department of Public Health. 1995. Web. May 2014.

Greenaction for Health and Environmental Justice. Web. June 2014.

Haraway, Donna. *Modest Witness @Second Millennium Femaleman_Meets_Oncomouse*. New York: Routledge, 1997.

Haraway, Donna. *Simiams, Cyborgs, and Women: The Reinvention of Nature*. New York: Routledge, 1991.

Haraway, Donna. "Situated Knowledges: The Science Question in Feminism." *Feminist Studies* 14.3 (1988): 575-599.

Harding, Sandra. "Standpoint Theories: Productively Controversial." *Hypatia* 24 .4 (2009): 192-200.

Harding, Sandra. *Sciences from Below: Feminisms, Postcolonialities, and Modernities*. Durham: Duke University Press, 2008.

Harding, Sandra. *Science and Social Inequality*. Chicago: University of Illinois Press, 2006.

Harding, Sandra. *Is Science Multicultural?* Ithaca, New York: Cornell University Press, 1998.

Harding, Sandra. *Whose Science? Whose Knowledge?: Thinking from Women's Lives*. Ithaca, New York: Cornell University Press, 1991.

Harding, Sandra. *The Science Question in Feminism*, Ithaca, New York: Cornell University Press, 1986.

Hoagland, Sarah. "Resisting Rationality." *Engendering Rationalities*. Eds. Nancy Tuana and Sandra Morgen. New York: SUNY Press, 2001. 125-150. Print.

Katz, Michael. "Health Programs in Bayview Hunters Points and Recommendations for Improving the Health of Bayview Hunter's Point Residents." Sept. 19, 2006. Web. May 2014.

Kournay, Janet. "The Place of Standpoint Theory in Feminist Science Studies." *Hypatia* 24.4 (2009): 209-218.

Lelchuk, Ilene. "Bayview Hunters Point S. F.'s Invisible Majority: Area With Highest Density of Children is Most Underserved." *San Francisco Chronicle* May 31, 2006: B1.

Matanoski, Genevieve et al. "Cancer Risks are Low-Level Radiation in U.S. Shipyard Workers." *Journal of Radiation Research* 49.1 (2008): 83-91.

Mohanty, Chandra. *Feminism Without Borders*. 2nd ed. Durham: Duke University Press, 2003.

Mothers Environmental & Justice Committee of Bayview Hunters Point. "Pollution, Health, Environmental Racism and Injustice: A Toxic Inventory of Bayview Hunters Point, San Francisco." 2004. Web. May 2014.

Narayan, Uma. "The Project of Feminist Epistemology: A Non Western Feminist on Epistemology." *Gender/Body/Knowledge*. Eds. Susan Bordo and Alison Jaggar. New Brunswick: Rutgers University Press, 1989. 213-224.

National Cancer Institute Long Island Breast Cancer Study Project, Past Initiatives. Web. June 2014.

National Cancer Institute SEER Stat Fact Sheets, 2011. Web. June 2014.

Pohlhaus, Gaile. "Knowing Communities: An Investigation of

Harding's Standpoint Epistemology." *Social Epistemology* 16.3 (2002): 283-293.

Sandoval, Chela. *The Methodology of the Oppressed.* Minneapolis: University of Minnesota Press, 2000.

Temple, James. "After Years, Bayview Will Finally Get Full-Service Grocery Store." *San Francisco Chronicle* December 12, 2007. Web. May 2014.

Tsing, Anna Lowenhoupt. *Friction: An Ethnography of Global Connection.* Princeton: Princeton University Press, 2004.

Wing, S., et al. "A Reevaluation of Cancer Incidence Near the Three Mile Island Nuclear Plant: The Collision of Evidence and Assumptions." *Environmental Health Perspectives* 105 (1997): 52-57. Print.

Zhou, Hongning, et al. "Radiation Risk to Low Fluences of Particles May Be Geater Than We Thought." *Proceedings of the National Academy of Sciences* 98.25 (2001): 14410-14415. Print.

Living My Material

An Interview with Dr. Patricia Hill Collins

KAILA ADIA STORY

ON NOVEMBER 22, 2013, I got a chance to sit down with Dr. Patricia Hill Collins, Distinguished University Professor of Sociology at the University of Maryland, College Park, about her research and publications on Motherhood as praxis, an institution, and a lived experience.

Kaila: In 2011, I served as a keynote speaker for the Motherhood Initiative for Research and Community Involvement (MIRCI) annual conference, "International Conference on Mothering, Education, and Maternal Pedagogies in Toronto, Canada. After the conference, Demeter Press, (the publishing arm of the MIRCI), approached me to edit a volume in honor of your work on motherhood. We have had a number of contributions on your many theories, like "othermothering," and the conception of u women's labor in the home and in the workplace. So we can go ahead and begin the interview. In your chapter, "Work, Family, and Black Women's Oppression," in your seminal book, *Black Feminist Thought: Knowledge, Consciousness, and the Politics of Empowerment,* you argue that black women's unpaid family labor is simultaneously confining and empowering for black women. Could you elaborate on this?

Patricia: When I originally wrote *Black Feminist Thought*, I was really talking about African American families, as they were organized in the '80s, and how they were responding to many of the social, political, and economic challenges that faced them up until that time. I pointed out that African American women, as mothers, were carrying a heavier load; they were doing unpaid labor and paid labor, this was the whole story of African American women always having to work outside the home, and also being responsible for work inside the home. That particular argument resonated with feminist scholarship of the time, in that, they were really trying to highlight, and make visible, the unpaid labor of all women; but at that time, feminist scholarship wasn't necessarily looking at the broader labor market in terms of hierarchies of women; Who was doing what kinds of work for pay in the labor market? I was much more in line with, both the history of African America's who assumed that the work black women did for their families came naturally, as opposed to seeing that as a second shift. At the same time, I was also more in tune with feminist scholarship that was arguing, that we also needed to look at unpaid labor. But I was critiquing both discourses.

I was critiquing the African American discourse that was saying: motherhood and black women are so strong that they can do everything forever. And I was also critiquing, the feminist scholarship that made invisible black women's work in the labor market by seeing it as somewhat naturalized. So the goal, in talking about motherhood, at that point in time, was not to see motherhood as a role that all women love to do, and want to do and would do willingly; But a role, or a set behaviors and practices, that were situated within a particular social context. I say this on the front end because as the social context has changed, so has that particular role and at the time, I also wanted to broaden the definition of motherhood. To see it not, just as one on one relationship between a woman and her child or children, but to see it as a political role.

There are political dimensions to motherhood, especially for African American women, and African American women understood, on some levels, that is exactly what they were doing. They were preparing their children to go out into a world that did not want them to be fully human, which is a political statement, and these women understood that motherhood was a site where politics happened. So, I was attempting to broaden the definition of motherhood, and the construct of othermothering that is attached to that. Because along with this, is the notion that if you are othermothering, you are thinking about the community's children.

For black women this operates as a sort of collective ethos, and their contributions and responsibilities for the African American's community and youth. Those ideas, I think, are very important and valuable.

The question that you are asking me, among many of the questions that you asked here, is how has that changed to now? I think what we are looking at now is African American women, as mothers, picking up even more of the responsibilities now, than was the case in the '80s and '90s because of the assault on black youth. We have to take mass incarceration very seriously, and that is something that was not in place in the 80s. Looking back, you can see the decade of the '80s as a transitional decade. I think what we are seeing now is black women, in a lot of ways, picking up the slack of responding to mass incarceration, and all that goes with that, in terms of their ability to find a partner, drugs sales and/or use as being the reason for mass incarceration, etc.

The social problems that are now in African American communities aren't inherent to the culture in the way that people want to depict them. They are problems that go along with changes, changes in capitalism, changes in sexism, changes in heterosexism, so we are living in a very different world now. So, what that means is the relationship between unpaid and paid labor has shifted in ways that I think present new challenges to African American women who are actual mothers, but who are also involved in othermothering functions. I think we also now have to come to terms with the fact that there are black women out there who do not see this inherent connection. There is a rupture from these traditions to now, so they would view the world quiet differently. That is the moment where I think we are.

Kaila: You mention mass incarceration and the assault on black youth, especially now, in light of new media, (Facebook, Twitter, Tumblr, and other social networks), we had the Trayvon Martin cyber campaigns for justice, reports, and pictures of the Zimmerman trial. More recently, with the cases of Renisha McBride, and others incidents where young black people are either asking for help, or walking down the street, they have been automatically assumed to be criminal in some way, and then murdered and/or assaulted. As I view social media, a lot of people who are discussing these things, are black women themselves. They are academics, professors, bloggers, etc, and they are all seeking justice for these kids; kids that they view as their own kids. And to echo what you were saying about othermothering, these women don't necessarily have children themselves in a sense, but they have students or friends with kids, that they see as their children. Do you see othermothering as a hindrance for black women, if you do at all? Or do you see it as something that is necessary and empowering for our community?

Patricia: I think it depends on the social context; you can take a set of ideas like othermothering, and ask what context is it being used in? And toward what end is it being used? and by which people? So, for example, if you are looking at African American communities, and the issue is to protect black children and black youth, othermothering is alive and well. There are people out there fighting the good fight, they are just not recognized as such. So the way that I described othermothering in the '80s and earlier, when black women took care of other people's kids, now an example of this, may be these women who take in foster kids, or in a variety of ways have to work with the state often now, as opposed to taking in their own relatives. But there are still lots of cases where people are picking up the slack. When it comes to African American communities themselves, these communities look very different than before.

We have to understand that class stratification has really had an impact on African American communities. They don't look like what they once did, when I grew up in them, when you had everyone in the same community, which fosters a certain kind of solidarity. You can be in a community that is really desperate in terms of services, in terms of people, in terms of resources, a community where you know you're struggling. You can be in a working class community that is really on the edge. You can be in a very affluent middle-class black community, where the kids are just wondering, "what it means for me to be black?" those are very different questions than how am I going to get breakfast? Or will I get killed on the way to school? So if we look at the mothering that occurs, or the othermothering that occurs, in those different communities, I would argue that you see less mothering the more up the scale, in terms of social class, one goes. Unless, you have people who are socially mobile, and have access to these ideas. So part of the question is, is othermothering still needed for African American politics and political advancement? And I would say, definitely, yes.

At the same time, othermothering in the context of the academy may be something that the academy realizes that it can somehow take this traditional ethos of unpaid labor. and get black women to do unpaid labor, for the school, without paying them. So my motto has always been "one paycheck, one job. Not one paycheck, two jobs." If the institution can find a way to exploit African American women's inclinations towards othermothering, and remix it within those particular traditions, why wouldn't it do that? So we have to be very careful around discourses of mentoring where the assumption is that only black women can mentor black kids, or black women can do it better than everyone else. I don't see that as othermothering, I see that as putting black women in a mammy role, which basically says that's what we want you to be. If they called it "Mammy," everybody would understand the combination of emotional labor, physical labor and exploitation; they would see that. But if we call it othermothering and mentoring, it sounds nicer, it also sounds like one is getting to actual cache for doing this historic work, without realizing that this is not necessarily the same thing.

So, backing up, I would say that if we look at African American women in particular, (and by the way African American women are not the only group that uses these ideas), these ideas go beyond African American communities. However, in my work, I focus on the forms that this takes for African American women, so while I am speaking from that this location, I am also speaking to broader issues. I think this is a very powerful site that needs to be claimed. Not as a biological function solely, but as a way in which we look to the collective and say: "if you care about your kids, there are certain things you have to do, and who are your kids? Are your kids just the ones that look like you? No. Are your kids the ones who you gave birth to? No." and quite frankly if the country looked at children and cared for children the way it claims to do, we would have a much more expanded notion of what othermothering actually is.

Kaila: You have written extensively about pop culture, more specifically about African American women within pop culture; how they are and/or have been depicted and viewed. With the emergence of reality television, and its depiction of motherhood as a praxis and institution, with shows like *Real Housewives of Atlanta* and *Basketball Wives* what messages do you think these shows are transmitting to audiences about motherhood in general? And black motherhood specifically?

Patricia: This is what I am going to confess; those are not the reality shows that I watch. Let me tell you why. I find those shows to be so market driven, only presenting the reality that audiences want to see. So when I turn on a show like *Real Housewives*, I can't even buy into the base concept of the show, seriously. We have been talking about black women going to work; we have not been talking about housewives. There are strong class issues with those shows. We are looking at really rich people, or really affluent people, and its not that they are not real people, that's not the point here. This is a handpicked group that is self-selected to go on television and behave in certain ways. I don't remember the exact name of show starring Bobby Brown and Whitney Houston, but I do remember it being a really painful show to watch. I think I only made it through one episode. Now if we look at the nature of that family structure, and the kids in that family, and what that is saying about motherhood, then it's extremely sad to me; for fatherhood as well. Men have certainly been a major factor here, and have a similar set of challenges for what they encounter in the media. What comes to mind immediately is this idea of a "Baby Daddy," and the women who are willing to get on TV and yell and scream insistently, and these aren't just young black women, they are also young white women as well. So this is the fusion, this reveals the more slippery boundaries of race now; where white women can become blackened by acting how stereotypical black women are expected to act.

Kaila: You also wrote in your book, *From Black Power to Hip Hop: Racism, Nationalism, and Feminism,* about how the New Racism has impacted the lives of black women. Could you discuss how New Racism has shaped motherhood for black women and other women of color?

Patricia: This is a huge question; one way that certainly has affected it, is the growing significance of representation. Media representations and the power of the media is huge, because if they can convince you that person X, or group Y, is a certain way, it becomes easier for them to pass certain public polices, and to put certain practices into place. A good example of this, which isn't necessarily a mother example, is the stop and frisk law. If they can make you assume that the "crime" is inherent to the bodies of black and Latino men, then they are going to take proactive action, by stopping and frisking them, based on those representations. And not necessarily based on data or fact. Or the case with Trayvon Martin you mentioned earlier, if one can assume that a young black man is a criminal based on skin color and/or representation, they are immediately fearful to the point where they feel like they can shoot him.

So one element of the New Racism, to me, has been to create more space for negative individual and collective policy reactions against people who are seen as a threat to the individual, or to the state. That has really been the function of how black people have been positioned, historically, in the U.S. Now, for black women and motherhood, it really depends on class differences, which black women are we talking about? And who do we consider to be a black woman, in terms of motherhood? So that is the first thing, who is the black woman? Are poor young black women, who are in bad cities and are in bad schools? And are they watching all of this stuff, and thinking that is what they need to be? That is one whole group that is dealing with a set of representations of themselves, and social policies that punish them for how they behave.

For example, Nikki Jones writes this wonderful book, *Between Good and Ghetto: African American Girls and Inner-City Violence*, and in it, she does this study of girls in Philadelphia who are violent, and will fight with you; tough girls. This is the conception of young b lack girls. Those young Black girls are somehow inherently violent, and Jones unpacks that, and looks at their environment, and you realize that they are in very different environment now than young black girls in the past; so part of the New Racism, manifests itself here, in terms of representations and institutions. But as it manifests here, it manifests in other places as well, in terms of "hand picked" African Americans, being held up as role models for everyone else that is very confining. We give people the name "role model," for how they should be, without providing opportunities to be that.

For example, I love Michelle Obama to death on one level, but she is really the middle-class upwardly-social mobile African American mother with two well-behaved children that all people wish they could have. Let's be really clear that this is not possible for most people, and it might not be desirable for most people. There are many different family forms. We are in a time now, where if I had to think about the New Racism, that is about the politics of inclusion. You see the same distributions rich people, poor people etc., but the mechanisms by which it happens are not as clear as someone standing at the door and saying " stay out," it is much more about how to negotiate all of these different actors, in the American context, and to make sure they go and stay in their assigned places. It is really hard because that is where the representations become a lot more powerful and we don't want to drop the ball, and not look at policies and institutions, and how they are organized.

Kaila: Speaking of Michelle Obama, could you talk about how does class, race and sexual orientation effect the ways in which some people see others as real mothers and/or actual mothers?

Patricia: The state is quiet clear in which women it sees, and rewards as a legitimate mother and what it deems as an illegitimate mother. The state has had a real commitment in conjunction with religious institutions to posit heterosexual married couples as the consummate example of family. Placing them at the center of family, and then positing certain types of mothers within those particular units. Now, we are in a period of time where that is negotiated, where that is changing, in fact changing quiet rapidly, despite a lot of pushback. The important thing here is to get the state and the religious institutions out of the middle, and ask the question "what is good for the children". Because everyone wants to build these arguments about family and motherhood around what is good for children, and if they all would take a step back and ask, "What is really good for children? What do children really need"? Well, they need economic stability; so if that's not there, it is very hard to parent when there are no resources, no money, and no opportunities. What do children need? They need education; they need healthy parents who love them, whatever the gender, and whatever the sexual orientation of those parents is. And if the children themselves are in fact gay, lesbian or transgender, they really need parents who love them even more. It is almost as if we have it backwards, we start with certain assumptions about the rightness of family forms and motherhood, and assume that certain outcomes will occur, without first starting with what sort of outcomes do we want to see, and doing everything possible to make that happen. I really think the second point of view that I am sharing, is how many African American women have mothered all along. Because they have seen that the world is not going to be a comfortable place for their children, they have had to figure out what that means, and what to do to protect the integrity and the humanity of the child, of youth, and to figure out what ways provide opportunities for them. And that is a road of struggle that is not always a victorious struggle depending on what you are dealing with.

Kaila: Do you see new media as a positive thing for mothers then?

Patricia: I think the issue for me is that I rarely put a moral frame on all of this stuff, whether it is positive or negative. I think the issue is that we are always dealing with the social context in which we find ourselves, and it is this, that is going to either provide opportunities or constraints in terms of parenting. And when it comes to new media, we have a set of powerful tools, we know they are powerful, the issue is what we do with them, and who the "we" is. A lot of it is dependent on the individual or the person to say, here I have in my hands this set of powerful tools, and what am I going to do with it? I have this little cell phone in my hand, either I am going to use it to just talk about the shoes that I bought for my girlfriends? or the shoes I bought for the baby? The shoes that I couldn't afford, because I really don't have a college fund for my baby, but I don't care, and I want them to look cute. When we are walking down the street is that how we want to use our cell phones? Or do we want to use our cell phone in other ways. Let's say I am a spoken word poet, and maybe I can get my spoken word poetry to someone who is in a completely different environment, but is dealing with the same issues that I am dealing with. Maybe we can use global culture in that way? Maybe we can use those text messages in that way? The little phone doesn't have to be one or the other; it can be a variety of things. Or conversely, families that are scattered now, we live very scattered lives, and this has been an issue. Something like Facebook, and something like text messages, brings people together. Look at Skype! Anything with the Internet creates new opportunities for intergenerational dialogue that wasn't possible before. So, there are possibilities to network with other people who are in remote locations. I would love to see people who are incarcerated, whether that be men, and increasingly women, to have the opportunity to Skype anytime they wanted with their loved ones. That would keep people networked in ways that might help with reentry. So we have technology that allows for many possibilities, and that allows us to do things we once couldn't. We just have to beef up our imagination and how we will use it.

Kaila: Thank you so much Dr. Hill Collins. I really appreciate this interview, and I know Demeter Press and many readers will to. Lastly, I was going to ask, if you would be willing to share, your own experiences with being a bio mother, an academic mother, and now a grandmother.

Patricia: I think that what is happening to me is, I have been living my material for a very long time, and I have been thinking about it. The one question I ask is: What are the conceptual tools that would've helped me understood the situation I am in now? And when I was younger? Like having a baby? I needed one set of tools. Or when I was involved in community politics, which I really was, I sort of saw all of this othermothering as being so crucial to what I do. Or growing up in Philadelphia, and understanding that the neighborhood was raising you, not just your parents, the neighborhood was raising you; so all of these different points, being in academia, and seeing the need for the students.

At the same time, I have been very successful in academia, I have been to rise to the top, and look around, and see what it looks like from the top. I have been able to see patterns of exploitation that weren't clear to me early on. So, I was pretty clear about adhering to my "one check, one job rule," and that has been one thing that has really served me well. I have seen a lot of my colleagues in academia fall to the waist side because they fundamentally work themselves to death, that is the only way to sum it up. They have compromised their health. If you look at the stats on black women and health, you will see they are not good. I have just seen people who have fought the good fight, and we all know it is important to do that. I have really wanted to be a champion to anyone who is that position, and black women are really the drum majors to this, "you have to take care of yourself, because if you do not survive, you cannot help anybody else". So this tradition of everyone singing at your funeral, and talking about how wonderful you were, that is something that is harmful.

At the beginning, I started with this notion it is really important to be a strong black mother and do this othermothering, but at the same time, if it is at the cost of ones own survival, it is really harmful, and is too high a price to pay. There is a sweet part in the middle between caring about only yourself, and this immersion in these networks that are just draining, but there is this place in the middle. And this whole notion of mothering and othermothering needs to be situated in that place, and that is what I have aspired to do, provide some language for my own survival. As I sit back and reflect, I think so far, so good.

Contributor Notes

Kaila Adia Story, Ph.D., is an Associate Professor in the Departments of Women's & Gender Studies and Pan African Studies. Dr. Story is also the Audre Lorde Chair in Race, Class, Gender and Sexuality Studies. Dr. Story's research examines the intersections of race and sexuality, with special attention to Black feminism, Black lesbians, and Black queer identity. Her recent work "La-La's Fundamental Rupture: True Blood's Lafayette and the Deconstruction of Normal" in the anthology *African Americans on Television: Race-ing for Ratings* explores the contested persona of the character Lafayette, and problematizes mediated messaging around Black, Gay, and Male embodiment and identity. Dr. Story's other current work explores the intersections of Black Queer Studies and Pan African Studies; also feminist theory's relationship to queer theory.

Deidre Hill Butler, Ph.D., is an Associate Professor of Sociology and Director of the Africana Studies Program at Union College in Schenectady, New York. Professor Hill Butler's academic research focuses on the roles of African American women within contemporary stepfamilies and representations of Black middle class women in the Obama era. She has published articles in *Afro-Americans in New York Life and History: An Interdisciplinary Journal* and the *Journal of the Association for the Research on Mothering*. She is a lifetime member of the Association of Black Women Historians and contributed an article to *Emerging Voices and Paradigms*, the organization's 2008 text. She has also guest-edited a special edition of the *Journal of Pan African Studies (JPAS)* on Africana mothering. She is the birth mother of two sons and a stepmother to four young adults

Toni C. King, Ph.D., is an Associate Provost at Denison University where she also holds a joint appointment in Black Studies and Women's Studies. Her courses include women's studies, Black studies, feminist research methods and race, gender and leadership. Toni's publications appear in the *National Women's Studies Association Journal*, the *Journal of Women and Therapy*, and a wide range of books and anthologies. King's recent book: *Black Womanist Leadership: Tracing the Motherline*, co-edited with S. Alease Ferguson (SUNY Press, 2011) anthologizes narratives of leadership transmission from mothers to daughters. Her scholarship nexus includes race and gender in the academy, diversity in higher education, and relational psychology. She specializes in designing and conducting workshops and seminars: women's leadership, diversity and anti-racism, and organizational change. Beyond the professional realm, she enjoys yoga and writing poetry.

S. Alease Ferguson, Ph.D., LPCC, is the Director of Mental Health Treatment Services for Specialized Alternatives for Families and Youth's (SAFY) Cleveland Division, a national therapeutic foster care organization. She also serves as a Professor of Psychology at the University of Phoenix Cleveland Campus in Beachwood Ohio and Notre Dame College of Ohio. Over the course of her career, she has served as a social services program administrator, evaluation researcher, organizational change consultant, and curriculum designer. Her research and practitioner efforts focus on cultural diversity, relational psychology, and African American women's mental health concerns and resistances to social oppression. To date, her co-authored works have been widely anthologized in the feminist press. She has recently published an edited volume with Toni C. King, *Black Womanist Leadership: Tracing the Motherline* (SUNY Press, 2011). In her leisure, she is dedicated to the crafts of grand mothering, gardening, playwriting and community activism.

Karline Wilson-Mitchell, RN, RM, CNM, MSN, was born in Jamaica and migrated to Canada as a young child. She has been practicing midwifery since 1992 and currently teaches in the Midwifery Education Program at Ryerson University, Toronto, Canada. She has conducted births in Florida, North Carolina, Georgia and the Greater Toronto area, in hospital and home. Karline has attended the births of many ethnically diverse populations, including new immigrant and refugee families. Her research interests include international health and health policy, birth outcomes of uninsured refugee and migrant women and newborns, perinatal loss, cultural health beliefs, and mental health issues facing newcomer women and pregnant Jamaican adolescents. She serves on the Health Disparities Subcomittee of the Midwives of Color Committee, (American College of Nurse-Midwives), Ryerson's Centre for Immigration and Settlement, and the Ryerson University Centre for Global Health and Health Equity.

Vincia Herbert, B. SC., was born in Montreal, Canada, of Caribbean heritage. She is a third-year midwifery student at Ryerson University in Toronto, Canada. She served the Association of Ryerson Midwifery Students. Her background includes a Bachelor's degree in Biology and previous employment as a community outreach adviser at a university-based equity and diversity education office. Her interests lie in women's health, access to care for marginalized communities, and sexual health education. She recently participated in an observational experience at a midwifery-led birth centre in Port of Spain, Trinidad. She has also participated in a research project recording the narrative discourse of Black women's birth experiences in Toronto.

Sarah N. Gatson, Ph.D., Northwestern University (1999); Associate Professor of Sociology, Texas A&M University. Interested in Inequality, Race/Ethnicity, Law, Gender, Culture, and qualitative methods, with projects centered on how people organize themselves in terms of community and citizenship; the multiracial identity movement; race, gender, class, and citizenship in U.S. legal culture, historical and contemporary feminism, and new media community-building practices.

Nancy Arden McHugh, Ph.D., is Professor of Philosophy and Chair at Wittenberg University. She is the author of *Feminist Philosophies A-Z* and articles in feminist philosophy of science and epistemology. Her current project *What Can We Do?* provides a pragmatist feminist analysis of scientific research practices. Nancy teaches as part of the Inside-Out Prison Exchange Program in London Correctional Facility and coordinates a collaborative youth restorative justice project, The Restorative Justice Initiative.

Shelley Grant, Ph.D. (Queen Mary University of London), is a legal and political geographer with a longstanding interest in evaluating the remembered beliefs and performances that now inform the contemporary civil identities of multicultural communities in America and Western Europe. She draws from theories on collective remembering to approach her analyses on the divergences in legal and cultural responses to shifting family building norms. Her studies on the geographies of human reproduction critically consider the influence of social difference on expectations for democratic participation as well as on public and private acts of family consumption. These research interests are grounded in her diverse background in legal research, public policy advocacy and corporate business management.

Abigail L. Palko, Ph.D., is the Director of Undergraduate Studies for the Gender Studies Program at the University of Notre Dame, as well as an Affiliate Faculty member of the Department of Africana Studies and Fellow of the Keough-Naughton Institute for Irish Studies. She holds a Ph.D. in Literature with a minor in Gender Studies, and her research focuses on twentieth-century Irish and Caribbean women novelists, with particular attention to their contestations of motherhood as institution and postcolonial questionings of heteronormative sexuality. Her current book project analyzes representations of subversive mothering practices in late twentieth-century Irish and Caribbean novels. Her essays have appeared in *Frontiers*, *New Hibernia Review*, and *Textual Practice*; she wrote a chapter on the Philadelphia organization Mothers in Charge for Demeter Press's *The 21st Century Motherhood Movement*. Her courses explore gender issues in literature and motherhood studies. In addition to practicing feminist mothering in her daily life with her partner and daughter, she is thrilled to be serving as the 2013-2015 co-chair of the Feminist Mothering Caucus for NWSA.

Martha Pitts is a doctoral student in English and a Women's and Gender Studies Graduate Minor at Louisiana State University. Her research interests include black feminist theory, gender ideology in nineteenth-century American literature and culture, life narratives, and feminist pedagogy. She has presented papers at the Association of American Women Writers conference, the National Women's Studies Association's conference, the Society for the Study of Southern Literature conference, and Tulane University's inaugural Black Women's Health Conference. Martha has had freelance pieces published in *Gambit Weekly* in New Orleans and the *Washington City Paper* in DC. As a blogger for *Ms.*, she writes about issues related to motherhood, black women, and popular culture. Martha was a summer fellow in the National Endowment for the Humanities Summer Institute, "The Role of Place in African American Biography in 2011." She is also a storyteller and scholar for the Louisiana Endowment for the Humanities Prime Time family literacy program.